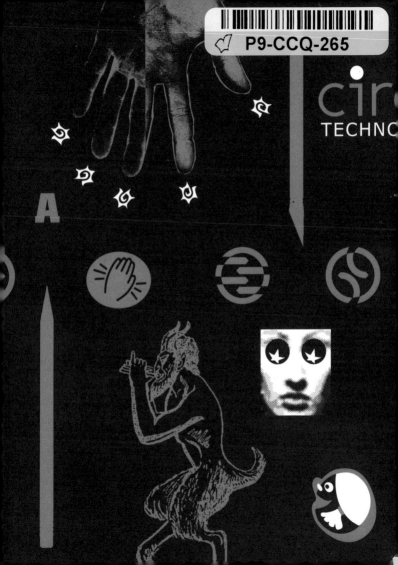

layout

brochure
poster/flyer
web design
advertising
newsletter
page layout
stationery

index

lay out

brochure
poster/flyer
web design
advertising
newsletter
page layout
stationery

index

JIM KRAUSE

NORTH LIGHT BOOKS
CINCINNATI, OHIO

www.howdesign.com

About the Author

Jim Krause has worked as a designer in the Pacific Northwest since the 1980s. He has produced award-winning work for clients large and small, including Microsoft, McDonald's, Washington Apples, Bell Helicopter, Paccar/Kenworth, Northern Trust and Seattle Public Schools.

Other fine North Light Books are available from your local bookstore, art supply store or direct from the publisher. Visit out Web site at www.howdesign.com for more resources for graphic designers.

05 04 03 02 01   5 4 3 2 1

Library of Congress Cataloging-in-Publication Data

Krause, Jim
    Layout index / Jim Krause
        p. cm.
    Includes index.
    ISBN 1-58180-146-7 (pbk. : alk. paper)
        1. Graphic design (Typography) 2. Layout (Printing) I. Title

Z246 .K83 2001
686.2'252–dc21   00-066833

Edited by Linda H. Hwang
Production coordinated by Emily Gross
Cover and interior designed by Jim Krause

This one is for my mom.

Thanks for everything.

Table of Contents

Table of Contents

Introduction

Lay: *to place; set forth for a purpose*
Out: *into sight or notice*

The Layout Index *is a follow-up companion to the* Idea Index. *If you own or have seen a copy of the* Idea Index, *you may be aware that it focuses on individual elements of a design (logos, images, illustrations, type). The* Layout Index, *on the other hand, is a book that offers suggestions for putting various elements together to form a visual message. Neither book requires the other in order to be used, although the two books could be searched in tandem for solutions and inspiration.*

This is not a "how to" book; this is a "what if" book.

Whether you are a designer, illustrator or anyone involved in the creation of visual material, this book assumes that you are already familiar (to some degree or another) with the tools of your trade. The purpose of this book is to augment these tools by providing your eyes and mind with a flurry of visual suggestions intended to ignite and inspire your particular style of creative output.

Not a typical layout book.

Most books about layout focus on the mechanics of arranging and displaying visual elements: alignment, proportion, relationship, grid, etc. Important considerations, for sure, and ones that are present in the examples shown in this book.

The *Layout Index*, however, is not a typical layout book. The "mechanical" aspects of design are not the ultimate focus here and are addressed by name in relatively few places. The examples featured in this book are aimed toward the intuitive centers of the mind and are meant to be viewed on a number of different levels—levels both conceptual and literal in nature: structure, arrangement, content, color, mood and more.

There is no "right way" to use the Layout Index.

If you are looking for concepts that could be applied to a specific project, allow the examples to strike you in whatever way they will—some may provide ideas relevant to your project, others will not. One or more of the examples may start a mental chain-reaction that leads to a solution that is a near relative to a concept seen here. Other times, a chain of ideas that begins here might end up far removed from these pages. The *Layout Index*, after all, is not meant to be a book of answers, but rather directions in which to explore.

Every person who views the samples in this book will react differently to what they see and use the material in a different way. Designers who adhere closely to traditional layout "rules" will, naturally, gather and apply ideas differently than those who employ more abstract criteria to assess their work. Students and new designers might find a wealth of fresh ideas on these pages; experienced professionals may see these samples as a quick-flowing stream of familiar visual cues from which they can consider and form new ideas. There is no "right way" to use this book, nor does it presume to tell anyone how to design, nor what is proper or improper. The *Layout Index* simply offers a large spectrum of ideas intended to spark the imagination of its viewer toward solutions they feel are appropriate based on their unique (and ever-developing) standard of finish.

How the Layout Index *is structured and why its structure can be ignored.*

The *Layout Index* is divided into eight chapters, each of which focuses on a specific form of media: brochure, flyer, Web page, newsletter, poster, advertising, page layout and stationery.

These chapters are meant to be regarded loosely. You might begin your search for brochure ideas in the brochure chapter, but it's just as likely that a sample from the poster or Web chapter could be applied—a concept from the newsletter section might apply itself perfectly to a client's stationery package. In other words, don't take the chapter headings too seriously. The creative sparks that lead to good solutions can come from anywhere (including the storehouse of ideas already in your head as well as an infinite number of other sources outside the pages of this book).

Where is the North Park Zoo?

While there may actually be more than one "North Park Zoo" in the world, the North Park Zoo featured in this book is not any of them. In fact, none of the clients featured in the *Layout Index* exist outside of its pages. These "clients" were invented for the purposes of this book so that design and layout ideas could be freely explored without being bound to the restrictions and guidelines that real-world organizations must establish.

The mix of pseudo-clients featured here represent an array of corporate, public, humanity and arts organizations. The samples featured for each client differ on a number of levels, including budget, scope and production parameters (colors, size, etc.). A broad spectrum of styles can also be seen among the examples (from conservative to "way out there"). The proportion of conservative, middle ground and out-there designs is roughly equivalent to real life—that is, less on either end than toward the center.

Most of the clients featured in this book appear in more than one chapter. As you look through these pages, you may want to take note of the ways that a client's "look" is (or is not) carried from one type of media to another. These comparisons may offer real-world suggestions for cross-media applications for your own work.

Focus Pages

Each section in this book contains "focus" pages. These facing-page spreads highlight principles of layout, client interaction and creativity that I have found useful during my career as a designer. Some of the topics are directly related to the content of their surrounding pages; others deal with more widely applicable ideas. Taken as a whole, these topics form a cohesive base of concepts that I hope will prove as useful to you as they have to me.

—*Jim Krause*

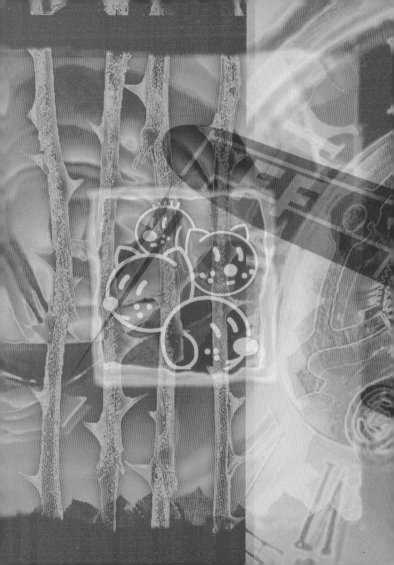

chapter 1

BROCHURE

BROCHURE

Brochure. A broadly applied term that refers to printed material, usually folded, sometimes stitched, sometimes with pockets for inserts. Brochures come in many sizes and shapes, and can (must) be designed to fit budgets large and small.

Brochures and/or Web pages often provide the public with their first view of a company or organization. It is critical that these sources of information portray the client in a way that is seen as advantageous to their purpose, both visually and content-wise.

Creating a brochure, then, is an exercise that uses both sides of the designer's brain: the right side must determine the right "feel" for the piece using both emotional and factual information gathered through various channels. The left side of the brain is in charge of practical considerations such as budget matters, production challenges, writing and coordination between other individuals who are involved in the piece's development and production.

This chapter features four clients' brochures. A variety of budgets, looks, formats and printing specifications are represented here.

Allow your mind to create it's own ideas based on what is seen here, don't hesitate to "stray" far from the specific material shown on these pages.

BROCHURE I

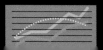

Growth
Financial
Services

OVERVIEW

CLIENT
Growth Financial Services, a corporation that offers investment opportunities for individuals.

OBJECTIVE
Create a brochure that will appeal to an audience with the financial means to invest in the services offered by Growth Financial.

CONTENT
The piece needs to contain a large amount of text as well as visual aids such as charts and graphs.

AUDIENCE
Upper-income adults, conservative.

PRODUCTION PARAMETERS
Budget is adequate for full-color printing with the potential for additional production effects such as die cuts, inserts and varnishes.

Brochure I

One cover (below), three potential interior layouts (right). A simple cover can contrast successfully with a busy interior, especially if there are "visual echoes" between the two (see pages 24–25).

EXPLORE AND CONSIDER:

NUMBER OF COLUMNS

TYPE/IMAGE RELATIONSHIPS

BACKGROUND COLOR

BACKGROUND PATTERN

BACKGROUND IMAGES

LINEWORK

WHITE SPACE

Contrast, exploring columns

Conversely, an active cover can be paired with an interior that features large areas of open space. Right: three possible interiors for the cover shown below.

EXPLORE AND CONSIDER:

COLUMN ARRANGEMENTS
IMAGE CROPPINGS
IMAGES WITH BORDERS
IMAGES WITHOUT BORDERS
VARIOUS LOGO PLACEMENTS
TYPE SIZE AND FONT
GRID/FREE-FORM
VARNISH EFFECTS

Brochure I

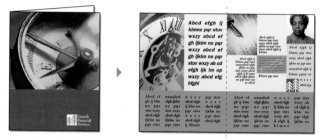

Consider designing a cover that complements, rather than contrasts with, its interior.

Explore layouts that incorporate more than a one-column format. How about using a variety of fonts and font sizes?

Limited budget or unexpected cutback? Most designs can adapt well to one or two colors of ink. Tints and screen builds (inks that overprint to create additional colors) can add depth to a page.

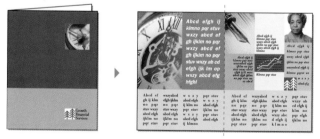

EXPLORE AND CONSIDER:

A PURELY TYPOGRAPHIC DESIGN

FONT CHOICES. ONE FONT? MANY FONTS? SIZE(S)?

VARIED OR CONSISTENT COLUMNS

REVERSED, MULTICOLORED OR LAYERED TYPE

TYPE EFFECTS: DROP SHADOW, ORNAMENTATION,
   BLUR, DAMAGE, OUTLINE, UNDERLINE

VARIATIONS OF "NORMAL" FOLDS

TINTS, SCREEN BUILDS, COLOR COMBINATIONS

Brochure I

A grid can be "softened" by breaking it up with headlines, photos and/or irregularly shaped graphics or images.

If a folder/insert design suits a project, consider the many ways that paper can be constructed into a folder. Talk with printers about options.

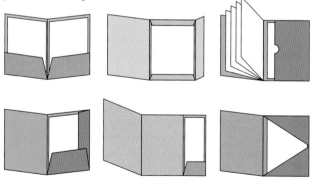

A visual theme can be established by using simple geometric shapes to contain or define images or typographic elements.

Investigate pocket configurations and insert designs that echo the cover and interior spread. Adding a tint to inserts can help set them apart from the brochure's interior.

At left, insert variations that also incorporate simple geometric shapes.

FOCUS ON

Visual Echoes

Music composers often introduce a theme early in a piece and construct the rest based on variations and explorations of that theme. Many designers do the same thing when, for instance, they introduce visual or thematic ideas on a brochure's cover and "echo" them throughout the piece's interior.

There are endless ways to establish and use visual echoes: a particular style of photography or illustration might be used as a common thread; decorative background images could appear throughout a piece; a particular grid or system of placement might be the theme that unifies a piece; a specific style of linework, borders or fonts could be used to establish a "look" that is echoed throughout a design.

Visual echoes can be subtle or obvious, visual or conceptual.

The following designs, taken from this section of the *Layout Index* feature two different kinds of visual echoes.

EVEN THOUGH THE COVER AND INTERIOR OF THIS PIECE ARE VERY DIFFERENT, THEY ARE VISUALLY CONNECTED THROUGH THE USE OF A COMMON GRAPHIC FORMAT AT THE CENTER OF EACH.

There are endless ways to "visually echo" elements and themes within a piece. Explore, investigate, experiment.

THE VISUAL ECHO USED BELOW IS MORE CONCEPTUAL THAN LITERAL: A BACKGROUND OF GHOSTED FORK IMAGES ON THE COVER IS ECHOED BY A GHOSTED AIRPLANE IMAGE INSIDE.

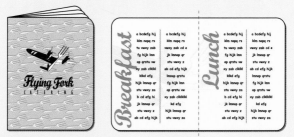

BROCHURE II

PETAL
BODY LOTION

OVERVIEW

CLIENT
Petal Body Lotion.

OBJECTIVE
Design a brochure that appeals to a viewer's emotional senses through artistically rendered symbolic images.

CONTENT
Message will be carried through a series of images that convey the transformation that occurs to the skin when this product is used. Text should be kept to a minimum.

AUDIENCE
Female, intuitive.

PRODUCTION PARAMETERS
Full color. Special treatments may be explored.

Brochure II

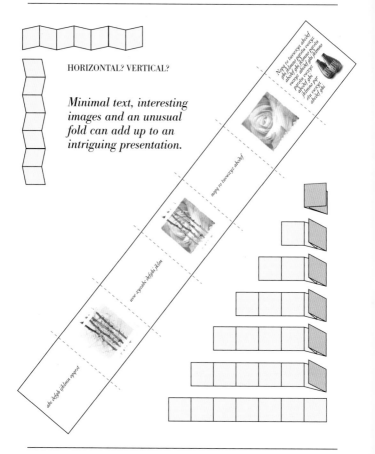

HORIZONTAL? VERTICAL?

Minimal text, interesting images and an unusual fold can add up to an intriguing presentation.

Tumble fold, speaking with pictures

Above and below, interiors that could be used with the cover design at left.

EXPLORE AND CONSIDER:
IMAGES THAT BLEED
CROWDED OR UNCROWDED IMAGES
UNUSUAL TYPOGRAPHIC ARRANGEMENTS

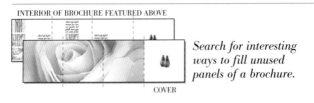

INTERIOR OF BROCHURE FEATURED ABOVE

COVER

Search for interesting ways to fill unused panels of a brochure.

Brochure II

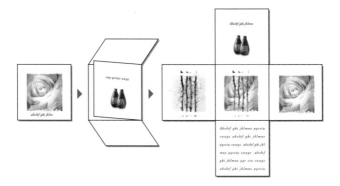

Search for physical characteristics of a piece that echo conceptual themes. The construction of these pieces, for example, mimics the blossoming of a flower.

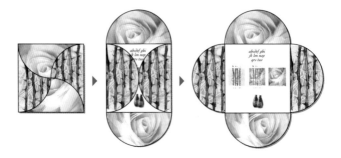

Other folds, image/text relationships

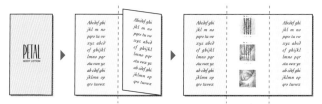

Persuading the emotions: unusual or shocking images, limited or vague text, interesting typography, poetry, lyrics, intriguing colors, blurred elements, white space, clutter.

EXPLORE AND CONSIDER:
THEMES AND/OR IMAGES THAT APPEAL TO THE EMOTIONS
DIFFERENT WAYS OF CONTRASTING OR COMBINING TEXT AND IMAGES
BACKGROUND COLORS, PATTERNS, IMAGES, TEXT
TYPE THAT FOLLOWS A CURVED OR ALTERED BASELINE
"FREE-FLOATING" TEXT
SONG LYRICS, POETRY, PROSE, QUOTATIONS, EXCERPTS FROM LITERATURE
"SOFT" COLORS, "HARSH" COLORS

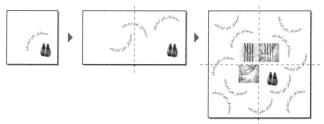

Brochure II

Consider a stitched rather than a fold-only piece.

EXPLORE: DIMENSIONS, DIE CUTS, TRANSLUCENT SHEETS, SPECIALTY PAPERS AND/OR INKS

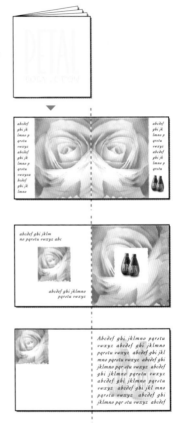

Booklets, unusual dimensions, text exploration

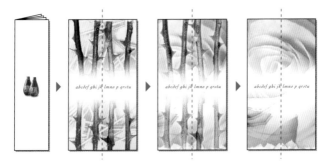

This page: extreme and narrow, multipage layouts

EXPLORE AND CONSIDER:
TEXT AND IMAGE RELATIONSHIPS
TEXT THAT INTEGRATES WITH IMAGES, TEXT THAT IS SEPARATE FROM IMAGES
LARGE TYPOGRAPHY, SMALL TYPOGRAPHY
EXTREME OR UNUSUAL DIMENSIONS
BUSY, LAYERED PAGES CONTRASTING WITH SIMPLE, PLAIN PAGES

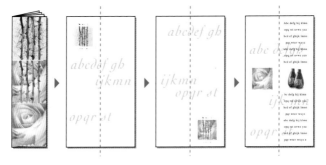

FOCUS ON

Folds

EXPLORE: SIZE, DIMENSION, DIE CUT, DRILL, STOCK, WEIGHT, ORIENTATION

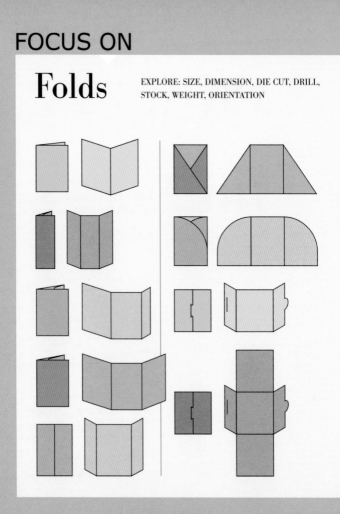

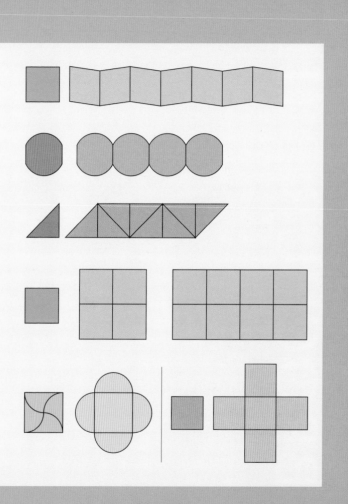

Flying Fork

OVERVIEW

CLIENT
Flying Fork Catering.

OBJECTIVE
Produce a simple and versatile brochure.
Budget is tight, artwork is limited to use of
the logo itself.

CONTENT
Information about the company along with
menu offerings for breakfast, lunch and
dinner events. Should have a "progressive
and affordable" look.

AUDIENCE
Contemporary.

PRODUCTION PARAMETERS
Limited budget. One or two ink colors
printed on a standard size sheet.
Thought should be given to designs that
allow information to be imprinted on a
per-client basis.

Brochure III

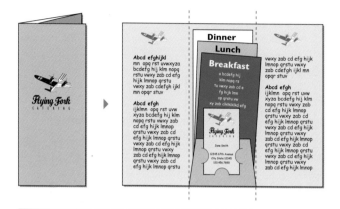

Above: Consider using screen tints to help create contrast between the cover, interior and inserts.

Combining multiple items on a single press sheet is a good way to stretch a budget. Talk with your printer for ideas and production specifics.

RIGHT: ONE SIDE OF A DOUBLE-SIDED PRESS SHEET THAT CONTAINS ALL OF THE ELEMENTS FOR THE ABOVE PACKAGE.

Adding a simple graphic element such as the starburst (above) is an easy way to create visual interest and establish a theme.

LEFT: A SINGLE-SIDED PRESS SHEET COULD BE USED TO PRINT ALL OF THE ELEMENTS FOR THE ABOVE PACKET. PIECES COULD BE CUT, FOLDED AND GLUED FOLLOWING THE PRESS RUN.

Brochure III

Investigate "looks" that reinforce an established theme.

The pseudo "passport" design used here ties-in with the logo's nostalgic aviation icon.

A background pattern can add depth to a design.

How about using vertical headings or otherwise "abnormal" orientations for text?

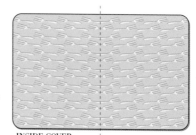

INSIDE COVER

INTERIOR SPREADS

Establishing theme, extending art resources

A FOLD-OUT DESIGN.
THINK: SMALL, MEDIUM, LARGE...▼

EXPLORE AND CONSIDER:
POSTER, FOLD-OUT FORMAT
LARGE OR SMALL
LOGO AS FEATURED ART
BORDER TREATMENT
BACKGROUND SCREENS
TYPE WRAPS
DROP SHADOWS
TILTED ELEMENTS
FLOODED COLOR
BLANK SPACE
LARGE HEADLINES
LARGE TEXT
VARIED TYPE SIZES

Brochure III

Consider using repetitive images, not only as a means of creating an interesting design, but also to stretch limited art resources.

A background pattern or image can help visually "bind" scattered elements.

Ultra low-budget and versatile: this spread features a single-color exterior that is printed ahead of time, and an interior that can be imprinted with specific content later using offset press, copy machine or laser printer.

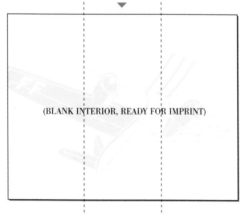

(BLANK INTERIOR, READY FOR IMPRINT)

LOW BUDGET AND LOW TECH
NEED NOT BE BORING:
EXPLORE OPTIONS THAT ARE
COPY-MACHINE FRIENDLY AND
GRAPHICALLY INTERESTING.

FOCUS ON

Brainstorming with Words

Although this spread may seem out of place in a book of visual ideas, it may be one of the most useful as an aid for coming up with ideas.

Whether you are just beginning a project, or have found yourself "stuck" while looking for a solution, you might find it helpful to read through all or part of this list of words—one or several of them could lead to a conceptual or visual solution for a project. As you read through the list, think about ways that the words, or combinations between them, could be applied to all or part of a layout. Allow these words and ideas to lead to others. Make lists of your own. Make a list when you begin a new project. Include words with your thumbnails.

LAYOUT	BLUR	REVERSE	ITALIC
ALL IMAGE	BUSY/PLAIN	SCIENTIFIC	LABEL
ALL TYPE	CARTOON	SEQUENCE	LARGE
ASYMMETRY	CHILDLIKE	SILHOUETTE	LETTERSPACE
BACKGROUND	COLLAGE	SKETCH	MONOGRAM
BORDER	CONTRAST	SPIRAL	OUTLINE
BLEED	CRUDE	SPLATTER	OVERLAP
CIRCLE	DAMAGE	STAMP	PUNCTUATE
COLOR	DARK/LIGHT	SYMBOL	SANS SERIF
CROP	DEFORM	TRANSLUCENT	SCRIPT
EMBLEM	DOODLE	TILT	SERIF
FREE-FORM	DROP SHADOW		SMALL
GRAPHIC	ELEGANT	**COLOR**	TYPEWRITER
GRID	FRAME	COMPLIMENT	THIN
IMAGE	GHOST	CONTRAST	
ILLUSTRATION	GLOW	OLD-STYLE	**MOOD**
LINEWORK	GRAFFITI	PRIMARY	ANGER
PATTERN	HUGE/TINY	MONOCHROME	WEEP
PHOTO	INTRICATE	PSYCHEDELIC	SHOUT
RECTANGLE	LINOCUT	UNITY	WHISPER
SYMMETRY	MINIMALISM		
SQUARE	MULTIMEDIA	**TYPE**	**ERA**
STAR	NEGATIVE	BOLD	FUTURISTIC
TRIANGLE	ODD	CALLIGRAPHY	INDUSTRIAL
WEIRD SHAPE	ORNAMENTAL	CONDENSE	MIDDLE AGES
	OVERLAP	CURSIVE	MODERN
STYLE	PAINT	CUSTOM FONT	NATURAL
BITMAP	PERSPECTIVE	EXPAND	PREHISTORIC
BIG/SMALL	REALISM	HAND-LETTER	RENAISSANCE
BLUEPRINT	REPETITION	INITIALS	REVOLUTION

BROCHURE IV

OVERVIEW

CLIENT
Animal Adoptions (nonprofit organization),
"Adopt a Furry Friend" campaign.

OBJECTIVE
Design a piece that playfully provides
information on a serious subject.

CONTENT
Textual content is brief. The message is
conveyed through a series of illustrations as
well as text. This piece is not intended to
fully educate its viewers on the subject, but
rather to encourage them to seek more
information by contacting the Animal
Adoptions center.

AUDIENCE
Young or old, caring.

PRODUCTION PARAMETERS
Full color with the possibility of "extras."

Brochure IV

A bc de fgh ij klm nop qrst uv wx yza bcde fg hi jkl mnop qr stu vwxy zab cde fghi jk lmn op qrs tuv wxyz abc de fgh ij klm nop rst uv wx

Yza bcde fg hi jkl mnop qr stu vwxy zab cde fghi jk lmn op qrs tuv wxyz abc de fgh ij klm nop qr yza bcde fg hi jkl mnop qr stu vwxy zab

abc de fgh ij klm nop qrst uv wx yza bcde fg hi jkl mnop qr stu vwxy zab cde fghi jk lmn op qrs tuv wxyz abc de fgh ij klm nop rst uv wx wxyyza bcde fg

Hi jkl mnop qr stu vwxy zab cde fghi jk lmn op qrs tuv wxyz abc de fgh ij klm nop qrst uv wx yza bcde fg hi jkl mnop qr stu vwxy zab cde fghi

abc de fgh ij klm nop qrst uv wx yza bcde fg hi jkl mnop qr stu vwxy zab cde fghi jk lmn

Adopt a Furry Friend

abc de fgh ij	bcde fg hi
klm nop qrst	jkl mnop qr
uv wx yza	stu vw xy
bcde fg hi	zab cde fghi
jkl mnop qr	jk lmn op
stu vwxy	qrs tuv
zab cde fghi	wxyz abc
jk lmn op	de fgh ij
qrs tuv wxyz	klm nop rst
abc de fgh ij	uv wxyyza
klm nop rst	bcde fg hi
uv wxyyza	jkl mnop

1-800-123-4567

Small-format booklets, spiral binding

Opposite page: three potential layouts for a small-format booklet. Note the "visual echoes" (see pages 24–25) between each cover and its interior.

This page: another idea to consider— spiral binding.

Brochure IV

At right: interior ideas for the cover design shown below.

Consider using background and/or border elements that tie in with an illustration's style.

How about a piece that folds out into a poster, suitable for display?

GO WILD:

ACTIVE BORDER TREATMENTS AND/OR DIVIDERS

TILTED TEXT AND IMAGES, CONTEMPORARY COLORS

UNUSUAL FONTS AND TYPOGRAPHIC SOLUTIONS

CUTTING-EDGE (OR RETRO) ILLUSTRATION STYLES

VARIED TEXT AND IMAGE SIZES...

Brochure IV

EXPLORE:
ODD SIZES AND SHAPES
UNUSUAL COLORS
INTERESTING PAPER
STRANGE TYPE

How about designing a piece that neither folds nor staples? Consider dimensions that have no right angles.

chapter 2

POSTER

POSTER

Most commercial artists enjoy the opportunity to design a poster. Often, posters offer the chance to push the boundaries—to do things that are not always "appropriate" for other forms of printed media.

Most often, a successful poster is one that delivers its message directly and powerfully through visual impact, an intriguing message, interesting colors, etc. Conversely, posters that fail or get lost in the crowd are usually ones that try to say too much, do not have at least one eye-grabbing feature or are simply too run-of-the-mill.

As you work on a layout, explore variations that bring one or another element to centerstage and then look for ways of visually and conceptually supporting that element. Experiment with designs that go "too far" and then pull them back if necessary. Investigate solutions that are image heavy, type heavy, colorful, odd, crisp, crude, dark or light. How about using blank space as a dominant feature?

Often, posters will follow the design cues established by other pieces—consider ways of adapting the material used in brochures, Web pages and flyers for use as poster material.

This chapter features posters for three clients; these solutions illustrate ideas comprising a wide range of styles and printing specifications.

POSTER I

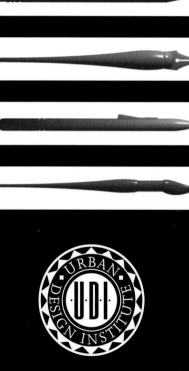

URBAN DESIGN INSTITUTE
UDI

LAYOUT INDEX.58

OVERVIEW

CLIENT
Urban Design Institute.

OBJECTIVE
Design a promotional poster for the Design Institute.

CONTENT
The poster should include all or part of a set of images that include the "tools of the trade"—both traditional and modern. If a single image is used, the electronic pen should be favored since it is most representative of the current industry today.

AUDIENCE
Artistically minded women and men, young and middle age.

PRODUCTION PARAMETERS
Experiment with two- and four-color printing, investigate the possibility of an unusual format.

Poster I

Placement is everything when dealing with white space: experiment until you are satisfied.

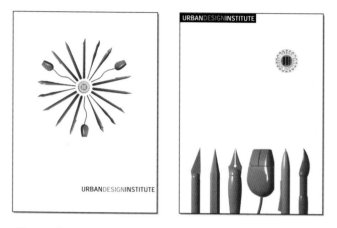

The two layouts featured above, though significantly different, are constructed from the same set of visual elements. Take inventory of available visuals at the beginning of a project and explore different ways that they could be arranged, combined, repeated, treated or layered.

All of the layouts featured on this spread are two-color designs.

Two color, white space, busy background

One way to draw a viewer's eye and attention to a poster is to give it plenty to look at. Below are two straightforward designs that offset a "busy" background with static foreground images and typography.

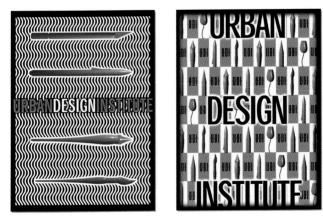

EXPLORE AND CONSIDER:
BUSY BACKGROUND VS. PLAIN FOREGROUND ELEMENTS
BUSY BACKGROUND PLUS BUSY FOREGROUND ELEMENTS
OP-ART. REPETITION
BOLD COLOR COMBINATIONS. QUIET COLORS
BACKGROUND PATTERNS: POP ART, OPTICAL ILLUSION, FABRIC PATTERNS,
    CHECKERBOARD, MULTI-IMAGES, LINEWORK, GEOMETRIC SHAPES

Poster I

There are many ways to fill and surround images with color.
Search for colors that connect with the audience and message.
Be aware of current trends in color.

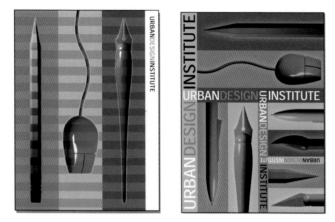

EXPLORE AND CONSIDER:
BLOCKS OF COLOR, PATTERN, IMAGES AND/OR TYPE
WHICH END IS UP? CONSIDER DIFFERENT ORIENTATIONS OF ELEMENTS
TINTED BLACK-AND-WHITE IMAGES
COLORS: COMPLIMENTARY, CLOSELY RELATED, HIGH CONTRAST

WHAT ARE CURRENT TRENDS IN COLOR? LOOK AROUND!

Color panels, black background

Two more heavy-coverage designs:
Left: repetition and symmetry as themes.
Right: the power of black.

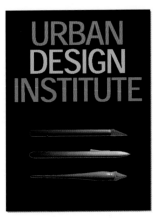

EXPLORE AND CONSIDER:
CROPPED IMAGES AND/OR TYPE
ELEMENTS THAT BLEED OFF THE EDGES OF THE POSTER
ELEMENTS THAT FADE INTO THE BACKGROUND
ELEMENTS THAT FADE TO BLACK
TYPESIZE: LARGE? SMALL? IN-BETWEEN?

Poster I

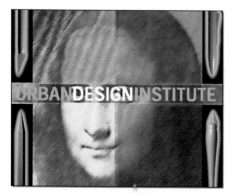

*Tried and true
or tired and
overused?*

*Would a play on
a historical
image be an
appropriate
solution?*

*Consider using a
historical motif
to emphasize a
message.*

Both of the type-heavy layouts featured on this page make use of the same set of elements: the range of possibility is endless when using words as imagery.

Above: type that has been heavily altered using software.

Left: linework and images provide the framework for this layout. Note the die-cut edges on this piece.

If the budget allows, consider breaking the mold by trimming or die cutting the poster into an unusual shape.

EXPLORE AND CONSIDER:
CIRCLE, TRIANGLE, DIAMOND
VERY WIDE OR TALL
IRREGULAR SHAPE
ROUNDED CORNERS
TORN EDGES

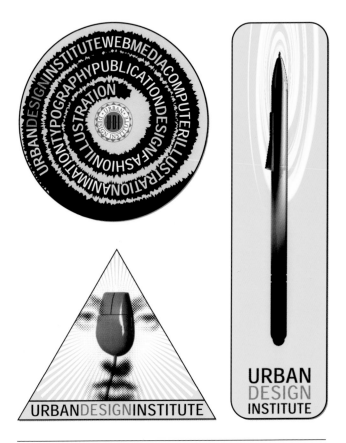

Drawing the Eye

Featured here are two designs that, although both potentially successful, attract the eye in very different ways.

The design below presents the viewer with three major elements (a solid bar containing type a circular logo and a series of tools). Each of these elements has a different "visual weight"—the eye moves comfortably among them as it gathers the piece's message.

The poster on this page presents a virtual wall of equally emphasized visual material. The attraction (for some) to this kind of design may lie in the fact that the mind's curiosity is aroused by the need to search and scan for a message.

Consider designs that incorporate visual hierarchy (left) or visual equality (below) as you search for a solution: be wary of designs that try to do both or neither.

POSTER II

FF

Flying Fork

OVERVIEW

CLIENT
Flying Fork Catering.

OBJECTIVE
Create a poster that lets people know that
Flying Fork is out there and ready to serve.

CONTENT
The main purpose of this poster is simply
to create name recognition for Flying Fork.
The image, therefore, should be bold and
memorable.

AUDIENCE
Wide variety of adults.

PRODUCTION PARAMETERS
One, two or possibly three colors.
Investigate cost-saving approaches.

Poster II

Cost effective and eye-catching. A large image can attract the eye regardless of whether or not it is printed in color. This design is printed with black ink on a speckled stock.

A single color of ink can be made to look like more with the use of screen tints.

Explore looks that relate to a relevant era.

The flag-like look of this design compliments the nostalgic feel of the logo.

Explore abstract connections such as this when looking for a solution.

This page: three-color variations of the single-color design shown on the previous spread.

Left: intentionally "out-of-register" inks.

Another variation: a simple, bold backdrop of complementary (or otherwise eye-catching) colors can draw attention to a poster.

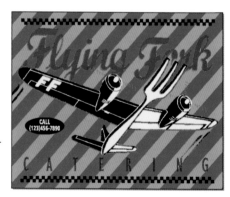

Three color, two color, heavy ink, screens

This page: one set of elements, two ink colors and two very different end results.

Left: an element from the logo is used as focal point. Heavy color coverage provides a backdrop for the image.

Right: making the most of a two-color job through a variety of screen tints, fonts, background and border elements.

Poster II

A simple message, simply portrayed. Would this approach work for your project?

Consider a handcrafted approach...

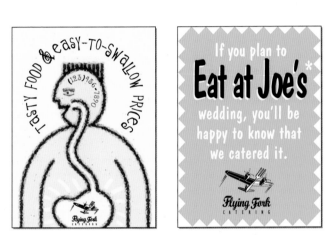

How about humor?

EXPLORE AND CONSIDER:
CARTOON, PLAY ON WORDS, SPEAKING BUBBLES, EDITORIAL COMMENTARY
ODD AND/OR HUMOROUS JUXTAPOSITION OF IMAGES

FOCUS ON

Type Legibility

Although some viewers are more tolerant of difficult-to-read type than others, it is usually important to present text with some degree of clarity. This can be a challenge when mixing type and images.

Shown on the opposite page are a few techniques that solve a difficult type/image combination. Make use of the effects and capabilities available through electronic media to explore these and other possibilities.

POOR LEGIBILITY: WHETHER PRINTED IN BLACK, OR REVERSED TO WHITE, THE TYPE IN THE SAMPLES BELOW IS DIFFICULT TO READ AGAINST THE BUSY BACKGROUND IMAGE. SOLUTIONS THAT OFFER BETTER LEGIBILITY ARE FEATURED ON THE OPPOSITE PAGE.

POSTER.79

POSTER III

thorn

OVERVIEW

CLIENT
Madlyn Portia, musician.

OBJECTIVE
Design a poster that promotes the artist's
new CD release, *Thorn*.

CONTENT
The typography and illustration used for
the CD packaging are available for use on
this poster. The look should be contemporary, edgy and somewhat moody. Black,
white and red should be favored as
background and accent colors.

AUDIENCE
Modern-minded teens and young adults.

PRODUCTION PARAMETERS
Full color, standard-size poster.

Metamorphosis.

The four designs shown on this spread feature a metamorphosis created using Adobe Photoshop. Any of these stages could be considered "finished"—it is up to the designer to decide when enough is enough.

Layering

The "layer" features available in Adobe Photoshop and other programs make it easy to add and remove visual elements until you are satisfied with a particular combination. It can be useful to go "too far" when searching for a solution—you can always simplify later.

Poster III

Left: consider a "classic" poster design—a full-bleed image.

Budget alternative: The poster at right features a black-only "threshold" version of the color original, printed on red stock.

EXPLORE AND CONSIDER:
IMAGE-ALTERING SOFTWARE
COPY MACHINES, LASER PRINTERS, QUICK-PRINT COMPANIES
BLOCK PRINTS
COLORFUL STOCK
NEWSPRINT

Full color, budget adaptation, repetition

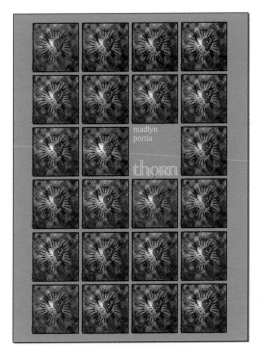

*Variation within repetition:
a simple means of creating
visual interest.*

Poster III

Typography and open space dominate the designs on this page. At left, large color, large type, small image.

Investigate interesting croppings and unusual image dimensions.

Right: lyrics from the CD appear subtly in the background of this layered design. Note that the white border lends visual relief to an otherwise image-heavy layout.

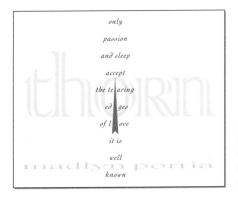

Consider a layout that uses only (or mostly) typographic elements.

FOCUS ON

Symmetry, Nonsymmetry

Two of the poster designs from this section are repeated here to serve as reminder of a consideration that is often bypassed by designers as they search for visual solutions: symmetry and nonsymmetry.

Some layouts are visually symmetrical: balanced along a centerline (opposite, top). Others are not (opposite, bottom).

Symmetrical design tends to be more conservative—"by the book." Nonsymmetrical layouts tend to be more "intuitive" in their construction.

Most designers tend toward one or the other of these two layout distinctions. Do you? If so, it might be interesting to take a look at the alternative as you search for ideas.

Explore mixtures of symmetry/nonsymmetry.

chapter 3

WEB DESIGN

WEB DESIGN

Warning: a fair amount of "techie-speak" is used in this chapter. If you are not familiar with words and acronyms such as *HTML, JavaScript, JPEG, GIF, load time* and *tables,* ignore them; this is a book about design, and the fundamentals of design hold true regardless of medium. If you are entering the profession of Web design and have not already begun to learn this emerging language, then you will need to do so, and there are many sources that offer in-depth coverage of these topics.

This chapter, therefore, focuses on Web *design,* and designing for the Web means working within a set of restrictions—ones that need not be viewed as limitations. Some of these restrictions are in regard to load time (the amount of time required for a page to appear on a viewer's screen), the Web palette (colors that are reasonably predictable from one monitor to another) and font choices (again, determined by machines other than the designer's). Explaining the many considerations involved in working within these restrictions, however, would mean to reverting to excessive techie-speak, so their explanations will be left for other resources. For now we will concentrate on the *layout* of Web pages.

Browse the Web to see what's new and attractive online; look through other chapters of this book as well when searching for ideas.

WEB DESIGN I

workflow

search and track

routing

data merge

communications

circle
TECHNOLOGIES

OVERVIEW

CLIENT
Circle Technologies, a high-tech firm that creates custom software for businesses.

OBJECTIVE
Design a Web site that features an entry page, a main navigation page and subsequent information pages.

CONTENT
The site should make use of the set of visual icons that identify the five areas of software development in which Circle Technologies specializes. The site should be modern, professional and quick-loading. Designs that depart from the traditional look of printed media should be explored.

AUDIENCE
Wide: from secretarial staff to software engineers and decision makers.

Web Design I

Consider a dimensional look. Experiment with buttons and other elements that appear to be made of a specific material.

The visual theme from the first two pages (background grid and metallic buttons) is evident even with the shifts in format on third-level pages (right).

Psuedo-dimension and material, visual vocabulary

*The "visual vocab-
ulary" available
for Web design is an
expansion of that
which is appropriate
for print:*

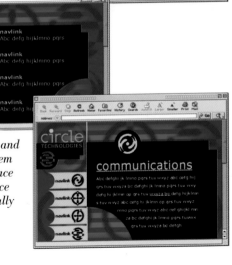

*...shapes, colors and
elements that seem
odd or out of place
on a printed piece
can work naturally
for Web design.*

Explore!

Web Design I

Consider creating pages that seem to have a tactile presence—one that encourages users to press buttons, move levers, adjust controls...

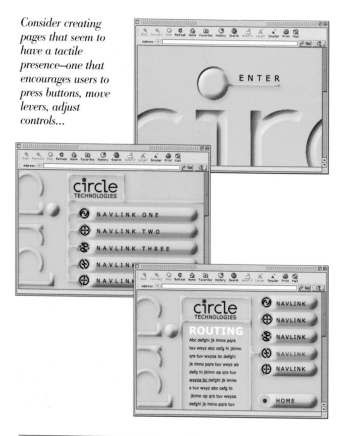

Interactivity, feel, continuity

Explore ways of establishing and following a theme without following it too closely. Note how these pages relate to one another in spite of their differences.

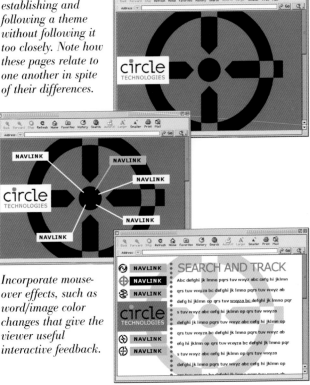

Incorporate mouse-over effects, such as word/image color changes that give the viewer useful interactive feedback.

Web Design I

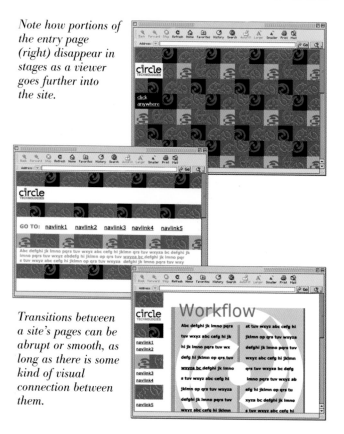

Note how portions of the entry page (right) disappear in stages as a viewer goes further into the site.

Transitions between a site's pages can be abrupt or smooth, as long as there is some kind of visual connection between them.

"*Electronic folder tabs*" *of some kind are very common on Web sites as an aid to site navigation: look for new ways of presenting them.*

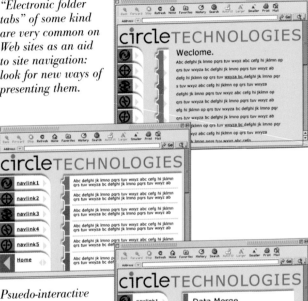

Psuedo-interactive elements such as these expanding tabs can lend a progressive look to a simple design.

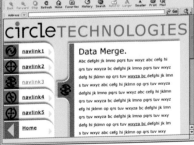

FOCUS ON

Web Realities

The information presented on this spread is aimed toward designers, experienced or otherwise, who have a limited knowledge of Web media. As stated in the introduction to this chapter, this book (being a book about design and layout) does not address the technical aspects of Web design in depth, but there are certain fundamentals that an artist needs to be aware of and investigate if they plan to work in this arena. Here are a few basics that are worth noting as an introduction to the realities of designing for the Web.

An artist who designs a brochure expects that, once printed, all of the finished pieces will look reasonably similar, if not identical. After all, printing presses are designed to achieve this aim. It comes as a surprise, then, to many designers when they learn that the Web page assembled on their computer may appear differently on another person's.

The reason for this is that the data that makes up a Web page is interpreted and displayed by the specific Web browser (Microsoft Internet Explorer, Netscape

Navigator, etc.) and the computer platform (Mac, PC) of the person viewing it. Fortunately, there are a limited number of Web browsers in use and there is growing agreement on how Web programming code should appear on different browsers/platforms. Nevertheless, it's a good idea for a designer to check their work for cross-browser and cross-platform issues by viewing their pages through a variety of browsers and browser versions, and on both Mac and PC machines.

Additionally, many designers create their Web pages so that they are sure to load properly on browser versions that are one (or more) removed from the most current version since it takes time for the public at large to upgrade to the latest.

These are just a few aspects of Web design to be aware of when entering the field. As a designer, you should also investigate the differences between using programs that write browser code for you (programs such as Macromedia Dreamweaver and Adobe GoLive), and learning to write HTML and JavaScript yourself. Keep an eye out for written and posted material concerning the latest happening on the Web: change is the constant there.

OVERVIEW

CLIENT
Urban Design Institute.

OBJECTIVE
Design a single Web page that contains a synopsis of what the Design Institute offers. The page should be visually rich without incurring an excessive "load-time penalty."

CONTENT
The Web page should feature three or four samples of student work that are representative of the school's major areas of focus for the upcoming term: Type and Design, Web Media, Illustration, Computer Illustration and Animation. The page could also feature some of the tools-of-the-trade used in the design profession. The look, content and colors should be progressive.

AUDIENCE
Artistically minded women and men, young and middle age.

Web Design II

Don't allow Web restrictions to limit the eye appeal of your design. Use small images, layers and interesting arrangements to compensate for the load time and color restrictions of the Web.

This design makes use of a background GIF image that, although large, is composed of just 8 colors, along with a scattering of tiny color images to create an eyeful of visual material that is quick to load.

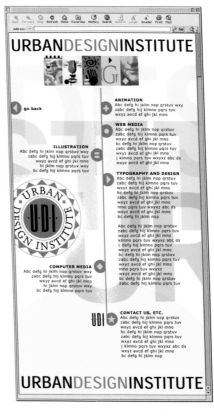

Although white is the background color seen most often on the Internet, consider alternatives from the Web palette (see pages 122–123).

Would linework help "tidy up" a design you are working on? Should the lines be broken up with visuals?

EXPLORE AND CONSIDER:
LINEWORK
VISUAL COMPARTMENTS
LAYERS
BACKGROUND WORDS
BACKGROUND IMAGES
BACKGROUND PATTERNS
BACKGROUND TEXTURES
TILED BACKGROUND
COLOR COMBINATIONS

Web Design II

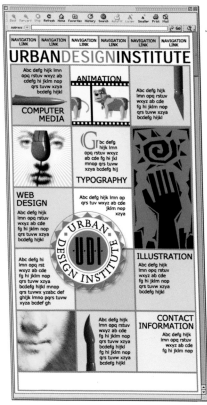

The grid used here is far more structured than the one used on the previous page, but the use of a variety of colors and styles within each compartment creates a visually interesting presentation.

HTML tables are very useful in creating pages of this kind.

EXPLORE AND CONSIDER:
BRIGHT COLORS
MUTED COLORS
CONTEMPORARY COLORS
DROP SHADOWS
GIF, JPEG OR...?
ANIMATION
SOUND
NAVIGATION BAR:
    TOP, SIDE, BOTTOM?

The purely free-form look of this design hides the fact that it, too, relies on HTML tables and sections that load separately (depending on their color-depth requirements)—allowing it to appear on the viewer's screen without too much delay.

Although the background image is a relatively small GIF file (considering the overall size of the image), it may load too slowly for many viewers—designs such as this will become more feasible as connection technology advances.

Is there a visual theme that can be "borrowed" from a piece already in use?

This Web page is based on the poster design featured on page 64.

The use of large type, bold color and intriguing imagery are as useful on the Web as they are on print.

The embossed navigation buttons superimposed over the 2-D background add a dimensional quality.

Borrowed theme, new theme, impact

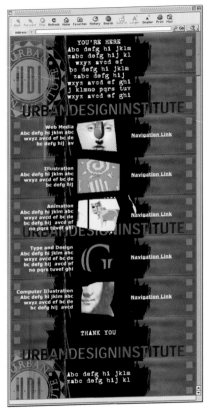

The filmstrip motif used here as a backdrop provides the visual theme. Explore conceptual and visual themes that could be applied to your design.

This background is composed of a repetition of horizontal "tiles"— an effective means of creating a quick-to-load, interesting backdrop to a page.

Small images, limited color, a tiled background and effectively written HTML can amount to visually rich presentations that do not make the viewer wait to see them.

FOCUS ON

Load Time

Simply put, if a page does not appear in front of a viewer's eyes before patience runs out, that viewer may be lost for good. After all, it only takes a click of the mouse to move to another site.

It's critical, then, that designers find ways of keeping the wait to a minimum—at least until load times (the time it takes for a page to appear on the viewer's screen) are reduced by improvements in Internet technology. A rule of thumb followed by many Web designers is this: *the only viewers who will wait longer than 10 to 20 seconds for a page to load are those who are either unusually patient or exceedingly interested in the content they are waiting for.*

In general, there are four factors for the designer to keep in mind when striving to keep load time to a minimum: the size of the images, the number of colors contained within the images, the amount of data contained on a page and the way that the HTML and/or JavaScript (or other) source code is written for the page.

You'll notice when surfing the Web that quick-loading pages usually contain either one large image, or of several small images (if they contain images at all). If you look deeper, you will discover that some images are saved in GIF format (best for images with limited color) or JPEG (usually best for more complex images). Talk with technically aware Web builders and look for books on the subject to learn how to design Web pages that use images that are sized, placed and saved in the fastest-loading format possible.

Another way of reducing load time is to control the amount of information that appears on each page. Break up content into several pages rather than trying to load everything onto one to reduce a viewer's wait. Note that an element that is loaded onto one page is "remembered" (and quickly rendered) by the viewer's browser if it is then loaded onto a subsequent page.

Also, learn from the pros and from books about how differences in the way the source code is written affects the speed and quality of its rendering.

WEB DESIGN III

OVERVIEW

CLIENT
Animal Adoptions (nonprofit organization),
"Adopt a Furry Friend" campaign.

OBJECTIVE
Design a series of Web pages that playfully
provide information on a serious subject.
For this presentation, show the site's entry
and a typical interior page.

CONTENT
The message should be portrayed in a step-
by-step manner. The text should be brief
but provide viewers with the opportunity to
link to more detailed information. The look
should be friendly and nontechnical—
a departure from what is usually seen on
the Web.

AUDIENCE
Young or old, caring.

Web Design III

Many Web users are intrigued by online devices that seem to respond to their input.

Careful planning of a Web page can improve load times. In this case, the TV, round navigation buttons and headline remain the same when the page's content changes. This cuts down on the amount of data that needs to load into the viewer's browser with each new page.

Psuedo-interactivity, anti-high-tech look

Would a motif from another era provide your site's viewers with a refreshing break from the high-tech status quo?

This design features a book whose pages seem to turn as the content changes.

EXPLORE AND CONSIDER:

BOOKS

SCROLLS

CHALKBOARD

HAND LETTERING

CALLIGRAPHY

GRAFITTI

CHALK

WATERCOLOR

PAINT, INK

SPRAY PAINT

Web Design III

Shown on these two pages are designs that contain all of their information on a single Web page.

Navigation elements can be incorporated that automatically scroll the viewer's browser to a specific part of the page.

Single-page design, quick and easy

The designs featured on these two pages are very straight-forward. The use of color, linework, shapes and drop-shadow effects add visual interest. Consider treatments such as these when searching for ideas when time and/or budget are limited.

EXPLORE AND CONSIDER:

BACKGROUND COLOR
BACKGROUND TEXTURE
BACKGROUND PATTERNS
LINEWORK
COLOR
INTERESTING FONTS
ADDED EFFECTS
SOUND
MOTION
INTERACTIVITY

Web Design III

Consider the audience's tastes when designing.

Image-heavy pages might be appropriate for younger viewers. Look for visual themes that also appeal to the target viewers.

Frames (windows within windows that can be made to scroll independently) are sometimes useful as a navigation/design tool.

The popularity of frames on Web sites rises and falls along with other trends. Advice: Use them if they are practical and can be made attractive.

FOCUS ON

Cross-Platform Consistency

Here, a closer look at some of the issues mentioned on pages 102 and 103—issues related to the aim of achieving a consistent presentation when a page is loaded onto one computer vs. another.

Color and font choices are, naturally, very important to a designer. Unfortunately, these elements are difficult for a designer to control when their work is viewed on a computer other than their own.

Color: Exercising color control on the Web means submitting to restriction. By sticking to a pre-determined palette of "Web-safe" colors (available for the choosing in most graphic and Web programs), a designer can be sure that, at the very least, their colors will not be dithered (contain an undesirable pattern of tiny colored dots when they are rendered). A typical 216-color Web-safe palette is shown on the opposite page. Remember too, that even when a "Web-safe" palette is used, there is no way to predict the individual color settings or accuracy of a viewer's monitor.

As far as fonts go, it is best to use fonts that are most likely to exist on a user's computer: fonts such as Times, Arial, Helvetica and Verdana. There are ways to upload fonts to a viewer's system, but this incurs an additional load-time penalty (see pages 112–113).

Headlines and other large typographic elements can be saved as images using any font a designer desires. The trade-off here is that while the designer will be able to control the look of the type, it will take longer for it to load. Many Web sites use a combination of type that loads as image, and type that loads as a font.

chapter 4

FLYER

FLYER

Flyer: defined here as a single-sided, letter-size, printed piece.

The purpose of all advertising media is to catch a person's attention and direct it elsewhere: to a product, event, concern, call-to-action. Flyers can be a cost-effective means of achieving this purpose.

Most flyers fall into one of two categories: those that point to something directly (an announcement for an event, an ad for a product, etc.) and those that point toward other media (a Web site, brochure, etc.).

The initial section of this chapter deals with the first of these kinds of flyers: those that point to something directly. These flyers are, for the most part designed as stand-alone pieces and do not relate directly to other pieces featured in this book. Some are text heavy, some contain mostly images, some reflect higher budgets than others.

The second type of flyer is represented in the second section. These flyers are intended to direct the viewer toward other media and other pieces. Elements from the media being "pointed toward" are used as the basis for the flyer's creation.

The third section features both kinds of flyers, all of which have been designed as imprints to existing stationery.

Every chapter of this book contains ideas that could be applied to flyer design. Keep a file of good flyer designs. Take note of the layout and production techniques used on publicly posted flyers.

FLYER I

CLIENT
Urban Design Institute.

OBJECTIVE
Design a flyer to announce the annual
Student Portfolio Exhibit. Flyer should be
printed in one or two colors.

CLIENT
Flying Fork Catering.

OBJECTIVE
Create a one-color flyer to advertise Flying
Fork's catered offerings. Piece could have a
tear-off or "take one" feature.

CLIENT
Madlyn Portia, musician.

OBJECTIVE
Produce a flyer to announce an upcoming
performance. Explore a wide variety of price
parameters for the piece.

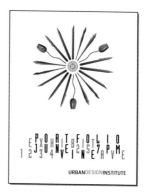

This page: two-color flyer ideas.

EXPLORE AND CONSIDER:

A TEXT-HEAVY LAYOUT
AN IMAGE- HEAVY LAYOUT
TYPOGRAPHIC COLLAGES
LAYERS OF IMAGES/TEXT

This page: black ink on a variety of stocks.

EXPLORE AND CONSIDER:
A SIMPLE, BOLD MESSAGE
UNCONVENTIONAL TYPOGRAPHY
LINEWORK
READY-TO-USE ART FROM OTHER PIECES
COPY MACHINE, LASER PRINTER
BRIGHTLY COLORED STOCKS

Flyer I

This page: a single color of ink, printed on a variety of stocks.

Flyers are most effective when something "grabs" the viewer's attention: size relationships, color combinations, interesting concepts...

Experiment by placing visual emphasis on different elements.

EXPLORE AND CONSIDER:
LARGE IMAGES OR TYPE
STRIKING COLOR COMBINATIONS
SCREEN TINTS
LAYERS OF IMAGES
BACKGROUND IMAGES
BORDER TREATMENTS
ONE FONT OR MANY
A "VINTAGE" OR ERA LOOK
NONLINEAR TYPE ARRANGEMENTS
INTERESTING BACKGROUND TREATMENT

Consider a "take one" flyer that allows viewers to keep all or part of a piece for future reference.

Single color, tear-off/take-home

Flyer I

This page: full-color designs.

EXPLORE AND CONSIDER:
TYPE-AS-BORDER
COLOR MODIFICATIONS
TINTED B&W IMAGES
GRAFFITI
"TORN" IMAGES
EXTREMELY CONDENSED TYPE
EXTREMELY EXPANDED TYPE

Large budget full color, low budget single color

This page: black ink on red stock.

EXPLORE AND CONSIDER:
ARCHIVAL ART
CRUDE TYPE
COLLAGE
CUT-AND-PASTE
VISUAL PUNS
HAND-DRAWN ELEMENTS

FOCUS ON

Font Compatibility

Using fonts from within a single family is a sure way of assuring typographic unity throughout a design.

Font families can also be mixed with good aesthetic results if done carefully. How is a proper mix achieved? Answers vary from designer to designer, but consider this suggestion: Avoid pairing fonts that are only slightly different from one another (such as the sans serif cousins, Futura and Helvetica). Instead, look for font families with obvious differences. The differences between fonts may be stark or subtle, depending on the desired end result—let your eye and mind tell you how much contrast is enough to ensure good relations between font families.

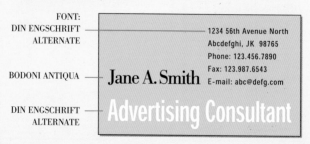

FONT:
DIN ENGSCHRIFT
ALTERNATE

BODONI ANTIQUA

DIN ENGSCHRIFT
ALTERNATE

1234 56th Avenue North
Abcdefghi, JK 98765
Phone: 123.456.7890
Fax: 123.987.6543
E-mail: abc@defg.com

Jane A. Smith

Advertising Consultant

What makes an old-style design look old-style? Often, it is the use of many compatible font families. Here, not only are the fonts varied, but a curved baseline at the top, vertical type within the piece and a variety of sizes add to the diversity.

FLYER II

CLIENT
Growth Financial Services.

OBJECTIVE
Create a full-color, two-sided flyer using art from an existing brochure.

CLIENT
Outdoor Adventures, Inc.

OBJECTIVE
Look through stock of existing full-page color ads for potential flyer artwork.

CLIENT
North Park Zoo, Summer Safari.

OBJECTIVE
Create a set of single-color flyers that print on the back side of existing newsletter art.

CLIENT
OutReach.

OBJECTIVE
Use an existing small-space ad as the basis of a single-color flyer.

Flyer II

This spread, adaptations of brochure art featured in chapter one.

Sometimes existing art can be used to produce cost-effective flyers. In these cases, a spread from a brochure (top images) has been run through the press, turned over and run again. The finished product is then cut, resulting in a full-color, two-sided flyer that is significantly less expensive than one produced "from scratch."

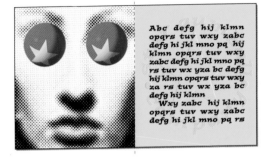

Flyer II

LOOK FAMILIAR?

The purpose of this spread is to illustrate the fact that flyer artwork may already exist for your project—the samples shown here are taken directly from the advertising chapter on pages 174–181.

Many printers, when printing a publication that contains advertising, offer "overruns" (extra copies) of ads at a competitive price. These extras can be trimmed and used as flyers.

If overruns are not available, the artwork may exist either electronically or as negatives. This art might be usable for regular offset printing, saving on prepress costs.

Flyer II

This spread: existing newsletter artwork used as the back side for a series of flyers.

Take a look at existing and past projects for flyer ideas.

In this case, extra copies of the newsletter/poster featured on page 225 have been printed without the back side. Later, the back side was printed with the flyer content shown here. The result—a series of flyers with reverse sides that could be used as wall art or book covers.

Newsletter/poster as flyer

Flyer II

This spread: art elements from existing ads used as flyer material.

Elements—and entire ads—from the samples shown on pages 188–189 have been incorporated into these black-ink-only flyer designs.

Take a look at available media: can certain elements be used as flyer art? How closely should the flyer resemble the original media?

An idea: Keep electronic or paper files of rejected or unused artwork from past projects—sometimes these can be used as building blocks for future projects.

Advertisement as flyer element

FOCUS ON

Voice

No pictures here—just words.

Words and the associations you give them.

Take advantage of the fact that our brains naturally link a storehouse of thoughts and images with words and the way they are spoken: *try thinking of your layout in terms of <u>voice</u>.*

It can be helpful to explore both the visual and thematic options for a piece by asking yourself, "If this piece were a voice, what would it sound like? Would it be yelling? Crying? Whispering? Seducing? etc. If so, what is being done to visually support this expression? Are all of the visual, conceptual and textual elements sharing the same voice? Should they be (or would a 'visual argument' make more sense for a particular project)?"

Once you've decided on the tone, character and content of a piece's voice, think about ways of translating this voice into a visual message.

It might be helpful to write down a word or a set of words that describe the voice that you want a piece to carry and evaluate your design against this theme as you work.

yell	*explain*
shout	*lecture*
scream	*laugh*
demand	*seduce*
beg	*entice*
cry	*mumble*
weep	*babble*
wail	*slur*
sing	*whisper*
chant	[silence]

FLYER III

CLIENT
Petal Body Lotion.

OBJECTIVE
Design a full-color informational flyer for retailers. Flyers should be printed directly on existing overstock of full-color letterhead.

CLIENT
Circle Technologies.

OBJECTIVE
Create a "dot-com" announcement flyer. Flyer should be printed in black ink using existing multicolor letterhead as stock.

CLIENT
Jane Smith, Advertising Consultant.

OBJECTIVE
Produce a simple flyer that can be printed on existing stationery using a copy machine or laser printer on an as-needed basis.

Flyer III

Above: four letterhead designs. Opposite page: full-color flyer imprints that visually echo the underlying letterhead.

A caution to observe when overprinting a letterhead that contains any halftone or screened images: beware of creating moiré patterns (an undesirable optical effect that can occur when the dot-pattern of one image overlays another). This can be avoided by overprinting only solid ink colors or by adjusting screen angles and densities. Consult your printer if you have concerns.

Full-color flyer on letterhead

Flyer III

Above: four letterhead designs. Opposite page: black imprints that visually echo the underlying letterhead.

The designs featured on the opposite page are designed to point the viewer toward another media: the World Wide Web. Print is still one of the most effective ways of directing people toward the Web.

Single-color imprint on letterhead

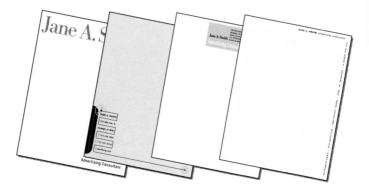

Above: four letterhead designs. Opposite page: black imprints that visually echo the underlying letterhead.

The predominantly typographic design of each letterhead has been complimented by a mostly type imprint. This (of course) need not always be the case, but it is an idea worth considering.

Many desktop laser printers and copy machines can handle this kind of imprint for short runs.

Typographic single-color imprint on flyer

chapter 5

ADVERTISING

ADVERTISING

A successful ad is one that captures a viewer's attention (sometimes in the midst of great visual competition), and then holds it until a message has been delivered.

There are many components that go into a successful ad and in many cases these components come from different sources: a creative director might come up with an ad's concept, a writer might put it to words, an illustrator or photographer could be called on to provide visual material, and a designer would then put everything in place—all of which would be subject to the review of still others.

At other times, a designer might be asked or allowed to put an ad together by themself. In any case, the definition of a successful ad remains the same—one that grabs the viewer's attention and delivers its message.

A wide variety of ads are presented in this chapter. The number of colors used, the kinds of production called for, and the budgets represented are diverse. Regardless of what kind of ad you are designing, look through many or all of the samples in this chapter (and others) for ideas. Keep a file of good advertisements that you can use as additional reference and a source of inspiration.

Keep your eyes and mind open to the advertising you see: What works? What doesn't?

ADVERTISING I

star gumball
company

OVERVIEW

CLIENT
Star Gumball Company.

OBJECTIVE
Design two full-color ads for publication in standard-size magazines. The first ad is to be full-page; the second, a vertical one-third-page format.

CONTENT
Since the age range of the target audience includes very young viewers, the ad's message should be conveyed primarily through images rather than words. The design should be colorful, high-impact and youthful.

AUDIENCE
Primary audience is grade school through late teens.

PRODUCTION PARAMETERS
Full-color, full-page and one-third-page vertical.

Advertising I

Ads without words:

Search for ways of conveying a message using symbols, colors and interesting backgrounds.

Explore ways of juxtaposing images to create a "visual vocabulary."

Visual vocabulary, sequential ads

This page: a series of ads connected through a common visual theme.

EXPLORE AND CONSIDER:
A SERIES OF RELATED IMAGES
THEMATIC SYMBOLS
COLOR THEME
BORDER TREATMENT THEME
CONCEPT/TEXTUAL THEME
A CONTINUING STORY
RELATED STORIES

Advertising I

This page: ads that make use of extremely limited text, bright colors and a variety of visual elements added to simple gumball images.

A three-part series of ads:

Ads in a series are often connected in some ways while being disconnected in others. Note the similarities and differences in theme, font, color and layout between these designs.

Advertising I

The layouts shown on this spread are vertical-format variations of ads featured previously.

By necessity, the ads have been altered to fit new dimensions. Take note of where the previous format has been followed and where it has been departed from in order to make the new design "fit."

EXPLORE AND CONSIDER:

COLOR BACKGROUNDS

ACTIVE BACKGROUNDS

WHITE SPACE

REPETITION

"SIDEWAYS" ELEMENTS

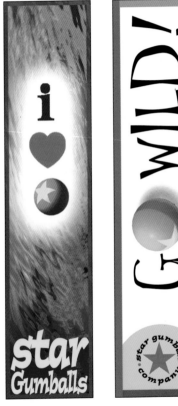

FOCUS ON

Placement

Layout is all about finding ways to fill an otherwise empty space, and a black dot inside a white rectangle is all that's needed to illustrate one aspect of eye-pleasing layout: placement.

So, what makes the placement of the black dot on the opposite pages so special? Consider this axiom: ***The most interesting place for an object on a page is one where the distances between that object and each of the page's edges are different.***

This axiom can be broadened: The height or width of the dot (or any shape for that matter) should not be the same as any of those distances. Going further, it could be said that no two measurements should be the same on a page: distances to the page's edge; distances between objects; dimensions of the objects themselves. Can this be done on a "real" project? Rarely, for sure, but being aware of the intrinsic "visual interest" in unlike measurements can be helpful in finding placements that are pleasing to the eye.

Learn this rule, practice it until it becomes second nature. And then break it whenever a layout can be improved or a concept enhanced by doing so.

Look at painting and design masterpieces. Notice how often this axiom is followed. Notice when and why it is broken.

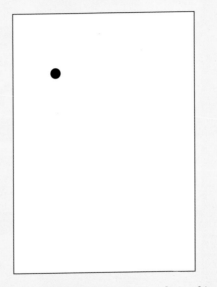

The importance of placement and size relationships cannot be understated. After all, once a piece's concept has been determined and visual/textual elements have been decided upon, most of the work that remains involves simply choosing where to place the elements and how big to make them.

ADVERTISING II

OVERVIEW

CLIENT
Outdoor Adventures, a company that organizes and hosts a variety of wilderness and adventure experiences for groups of physically active individuals.

OBJECTIVE
Create one ad and adapt the content to fit a variety of space allowances. Ad will run primarily in full-color publications.

CONTENT
Content should position Outdoor Adventures as an organizer of high-energy trips and events for working professionals in need of a break from their usual routine.

AUDIENCE
This ad is aimed mainly toward middle-aged professionals and should therefore have a look that is somewhere between cutting edge and corporate.

Advertising II

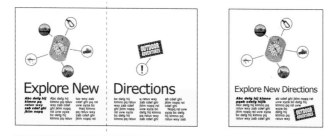

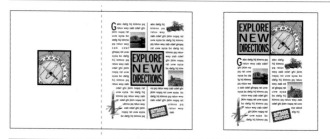

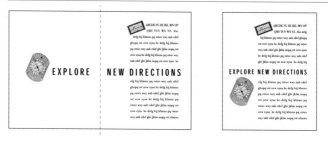

White space, continuity between sizes

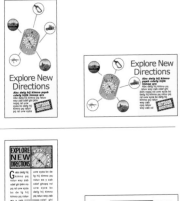

Often, a series of ads need to be created from a single design in order to fit a variety of media placements.

Note how the ads featured in this section retain and reject certain elements in order to fit within new dimensions while maintaining a connection with one another.

The ads featured on this spread make use of "white space" to focus attention on featured elements.

Advertising II

Image-heavy ads, continuity between sizes

Image-heavy layout ideas:

EXPLORE AND CONSIDER:

PHOTOS:
   CLOSE-UP
   PANORAMIC
   COLORFUL
   BLACK AND WHITE
   ALTERED COLOR
   "POLAROID" QUALITY
   OUT OF FOCUS
   EMOTIONAL CONTENT
PHOTOS THAT BLEED
PHOTOS THAT ARE CROPPED
PHOTOS WITHIN TYPE
PHOTOS WITHIN PHOTOS
ELECTRONIC PHOTO EFFECTS
LAYERS OF IMAGES
LAYERS OF IMAGES AND TEXT
THICK BORDERS
THIN BORDERS
"VISUALLY ACTIVE" BORDERS
COLOR BACKGROUNDS
IMAGES AS BACKGROUND
PATTERN AS BACKGROUND

Advertising II

Multipanel design, continuity between sizes

These ads make use of a multipanel design approach—a layout technique defined here as one where visual and typographic elements are contained within shapes, colors, borders etc.

Look familiar? This ad was derived directly from the newsletter design on page 204. Sometimes, art from a brochure, newsletter or flyer can be easily adapted to serve as an ad.

Advertising II

Black and white, continuity between sizes

Usage of a single color of ink—by choice or because of budget restrictions—can achieve powerful results.

EXPLORE AND CONSIDER:
STRIKING B&W PHOTOGRAPHY
PHOTO EFFECTS
PEN AND INK ILLUSTRATIONS
LARGE BLACK AREAS
LARGE WHITE AREAS
IMAGES THAT BLEED
CROPPED IMAGES

Even when full-color printing is available in a publication, it might be worthwhile to experiment with "restrained" solutions—layouts that use color as accent.

FOCUS ON

Image Cropping

When deciding how to present a image, explore different ways that a photograph, illustration or graphic element can be cropped. The software currently used by most graphics professionals allow for easy experimentation when it comes to looking at the options.

Consider shape, proportions, size and edge treatments. Should the photo bleed off the page's edge or be contained within the page? How about zooming in on a certain portion of an image?

ADVERTISING III

outreach

OVERVIEW

CLIENT
OutReach is an organization that connects adults with children in need through a program called "Give Five."

OBJECTIVE
Client has a limited budget: design should be inexpensive to produce and should reproduce well in black and white. Explore a variety of small-space dimensions.

CONTENT
The ad should contain the headline, "Give Five," and (space permitting) a single paragraph of text. An image of an open hand (relating to the concept of five) could be included.

AUDIENCE
Progressive-minded, socially aware adults.

PRODUCTION PARAMETERS
Inexpensive, black and white.

Consider creating an ad with no screens (gray shades)—these are easy and inexpensive to reproduce in a variety of media.

Strive to create a layout that draws attention to the ad and also helps it stand apart from the (inevitable) crowd.

Cheap art: the hands featured in these ads were "photographed" by using a desktop scanner and then manipulated in Adobe Photoshop (see pages 252–253 for more about this technique). Keep ideas like this in mind when looking for budget solutions for a project.

Advertising III

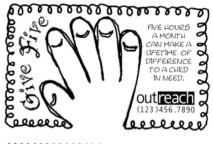

This spread: ads that call for attention through a variety of easily produced black-against-white illustration and graphic styles.

There are endless ways to display an ad's content, even when restricted to a single color of ink. Explore.

Black-and-white small-space ads

EXPLORE AND CONSIDER:
HAND-DRAWN ELEMENTS
CARTOONS
UNUSUAL BORDER TREATMENTS
LINEWORK AROUND AND/OR INSIDE AD
INTERESTING, BOLD TYPOGRAPHY
"SIDEWAYS" ELEMENTS
REVERSED TEXT/GRAPHICS

Advertising III

GIVE.
GIVE.
GIVE.
GIVE.
GIVE.

Give five.
Five hours
a month can
make a
lifetime
of difference
to a child
in need.

out**reach**
(123)456.7890

thank you.

Five hours
a month can
make a
lifetime
of difference
to a child
in need.

G5 GIVE FIVE

out**reach**
(123)456.7890

GIVE 5

Five hours a month
can make a lifetime
of difference to a
child in need.

out**reach**
(123)456.7890

GIVE FIVE.
Five hours a month can
make a lifetime of
difference to a child in need.

out**reach**
(123)456.7890

Type-only ads:

EXPLORE AND
CONSIDER:
FONT CHOICES
CONDENSED TYPE
EXPANDED TYPE
TYPE WEIGHTS
SMALL TYPE
LARGE TYPE
CROPPED TYPE

A small-space ad has a better chance of standing out in the crowd with a perimeter between the ad's outer border and its content. This can be achieved through empty areas (black space, white space etc.), thick borders and other visual devices. Look at publications to see what works and what doesn't.

FOCUS ON

Visual Tweaking

It is amazing how often a simple "tweak" to an element within a design can bring an entire page to life. This spread illustrates a few of the ways that an image (below) can be made to stand out on a page or stand-apart from other elements.

Here are a few ideas: enlarge, add a border (consider the *many* possibilities), tilt, add a drop shadow, add directional elements that "point," add a dynamic background, add a bold color.

Some enhancements or alterations are subtle, some are dramatic. Which would be right for your project—or, would it be better to leave things as they are?

NG & MOUNTAINEERING USE ONLY

chapter 6

NEWSLETTER

Newsletters, like brochures, come in many shapes, sizes and formats. Most often, a newsletter will follow established design cues set forth by other pieces such as a company's brochure(s), Web site or stationery.

When creating a newsletter, a designer must find a balance between a piece that informs and a piece that the intended viewer will find exciting, entertaining and/or interesting. The content of a brochure and the company's "feel" usually determine where this balance is to be found. Listen to the client carefully to find this direction.

One of the biggest difficulties facing a newsletter designer is the challenge of making things fit: words and images that fit into the space allowed for an article, and articles that fit *together* to form a whole. Making adjustments to type sizes, leading and column widths, as well as to image sizes and proportions are useful means of getting everything in place. The use of dividers and background shading can be helpful in creating visual division between the articles.

Remember, the examples featured in this chapter are only beginnings. Your solutions may be the result of several or a few (or none!) of the ideas presented here. Turn to other chapters and other sources for inspiration too.

OVERVIEW

CLIENT
Outdoor Adventures, a company that organizes and hosts a variety of wilderness and adventure experiences for groups of physically active individuals.

OBJECTIVE
Create a seasonal newsletter that excites and informs current and prospective clients.

CONTENT
Abundant images that convey the season's activities. Photos and illustrations of people, places and equipment.

AUDIENCE
Informed, physically fit adventure seekers.

PRODUCTION PARAMETERS
Full-color, self-mailing, standard-size newsletter. Could be designed as a single sheet or multipage.

Newsletter I

Relationships between cover and interior

Left and below: full-color layouts that offer suggested relationships between a newsletter's cover and its interior.

Should your design be visually active, static or somewhere in-between?

EXPLORE AND CONSIDER:
ONE FONT? ONE FONT FAMILY? SEVERAL FONTS? (SEE PAGES 136–137.)
WHICH FONT(S) RELATE BEST TO THE NEWSLETTER'S CONTENT?
COLUMN WIDTHS AND ARRANGEMENTS: CONSISTENT COLUMNS? VARIED?
GRID: TIGHTLY OR LOOSELY FOLLOWED? NO GRID? (SEE PAGES 214–215.)
IMAGES: CROPPED, FREE FLOATING, BORDERED, BLEEDING, LARGE, SMALL?
BLANK AREAS? LAYERS OF TEXT AND IMAGES?
BACKGROUND COLORS, PATTERNS, SHAPES, IMAGES AND/OR TYPOGRAPHY?
DIVIDERS BETWEEN ARTICLES? COLORED PANELS BEHIND ARTICLES?

TRY PLACING DIFFERENT DEGREES OF EMPHASIS ON A VARIETY OF
ELEMENTS UNTIL YOU ARE SATISFIED WITH A PARTICULAR ARRANGEMENT.

Newsletter I

Top and middle right: active interiors for the cover design featured below.

Bottom left and right: a mostly type design with color panels.

Active design, typographic solutions, image ideas

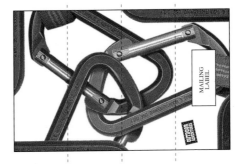

A single interesting element can provide an amazing amount of visual material: In this case, a photo of a climber's carabiner has been colored, cropped, rotated and layered to create all of the the images featured in this piece.

EXPERIMENT WITH USING A DESKTOP SCANNER AS A CAMERA: THE "PHOTOGRAPH" USED HERE WAS TAKEN BY LAYING A CARABINER DIRECTLY ON THE BED OF A SCANNER. (SEE PAGES 252–253 FOR MORE ABOUT THIS TECHNIQUE.)

Newsletter I

Look for other ways of separating the articles in a newsletter. These layouts make use of a "tabletop display" of objects, photographs and pseudo-notepad sheets that contain handwritten text.

Below, a two-color adaptation of the above design. The dark color of the text was achieved by layering the two colors on top of each other. A "posterized" effect been applied to the photos—an attempt to compensate for the lack of color by adding an "artistic" touch.

Multidimensional layout, divider ideas

Want to use dividers between columns? Explore options...

- Abc defgh ijkl
- mnop qr stuv
- wxy zab cde fg
- hi jklmno pqrs tu
- vwxyz abc de
- fgh ijkl mnop qr
- stuv wxy zab
- cde fg hi jklmno
- pqrs tu vwxyz
- abc defgh ijkl
- mnop qr stuv
- wxy zab cde fg
- hi jklmno pqrs tu
- vwxyz abc def
- gh ijkl mnop qr
- stuv wxy zab
- cde fg hi jklmno
- pqrs tu vwxyz

★ Abc defgh ijkl
★ mnop qr stuv
★ wxy zab cde fg
★ hi jklmno pqrs tu
★ vwxyz abc de
  fgh ijkl mnop qr
  stuv wxy zab
★ cde fg hi jklmno
  pqrs tu vwxyz
  abc defgh ijkl
★ mnop qr stuv
  wxy zab cde fg
★ hi jklmno pqrs tu
★ vwxyz abc def
  gh ijkl mnop qr
★ stuv wxy zab
  cde fg hi jklmno
★ pqrs tu vwxyz

Abc defgh ijkl
mnop qr stuv
wxy zab cde fg
hi jklmno pqrs tu
vwxyz abc de
fgh ijkl mnop qr
stuv wxy zab
cde fg hi jklmno
pqrs tu vwxyz
abc defgh ijkl
mnop qr stuv
wxy zab cde fg
hi jklmno pqrs tu
vwxyz abc def
gh ijkl mnop qr
stuv wxy zab
cde fg hi jklmno
pqrs tu vwxyz

Abc defgh ijkl
mnop qr stuv
wxy zab cde fg
hi jklmno pqrs tu
vwxyz abc de
fgh ijkl mnop qr
stuv wxy zab
cde fg hi jklmno
pqrs tu vwxyz
abc defgh ijkl
mnop qr stuv
wxy zab cde fg
hi jklmno pqrs tu
vwxyz abc def
gh ijkl mnop qr
stuv wxy zab
cde fg hi jklmno
pqrs tu vwxyz

Abc defgh ijkl
mnop qr stuv
wxy zab cde fg
hi jklmno pqrs tu
vwxyz abc de
fgh ijkl mnop qr
stuv wxy zab
cde fg hi jklmno
pqrs tu vwxyz
abc defgh ijkl
mnop qr stuv
wxy zab cde fg
hi jklmno pqrs tu
vwxyz abc def
gh ijkl mnop qr
stuv wxy zab
cde fg hi jklmno
pqrs tu vwxyz

Abc defgh ijkl
mnop qr stuv
wxy zab cde fg
hi jklmno pqrs tu
vwxyz abc de
fgh ijkl mnop qr
stuv wxy zab
cde fg hi jklmno
pqrs tu vwxyz
abc defgh ijkl
mnop qr stuv
wxy zab cde fg
hi jklmno pqrs tu
vwxyz abc def
gh ijkl mnop qr
stuv wxy zab
cde fg hi jklmno
pqrs tu vwxyz

Abc defgh ijkl
mnop qr stuv
wxy zab cde fg
hi jklmno pqrs tu
vwxyz abc de
fgh ijkl mnop qr
stuv wxy zab
cde fg hi jklmno
pqrs tu vwxyz
abc defgh ijkl
mnop qr stuv
wxy zab cde fg
hi jklmno pqrs tu
vwxyz abc def
gh ijkl mnop qr
stuv wxy zab
cde fg hi jklmno
pqrs tu vwxyz

Abc defgh ijkl
mnop qr stuv
wxy zab cde fg
hi jklmno pqrs tu
vwxyz abc de
fgh ijkl mnop qr
stuv wxy zab
cde fg hi jklmno
pqrs tu vwxyz
abc defgh ijkl
mnop qr stuv
wxy zab cde fg
hi jklmno pqrs tu
vwxyz abc def
gh ijkl mnop qr
stuv wxy zab
cde fg hi jklmno
pqrs tu vwxyz

Abc defgh ijkl
mnop qr stuv
wxy zab cde fg
hi jklmno pqrs tu
vwxyz abc de
fgh ijkl mnop qr
stuv wxy zab
cde fg hi jklmno
pqrs tu vwxyz
abc defgh ijkl
mnop qr stuv
wxy zab cde fg
hi jklmno pqrs tu
vwxyz abc def
gh ijkl mnop qr
stuv wxy zab
cde fg hi jklmno
pqrs tu vwxyz

Abc defgh ijkl
mnop qr stuv
wxy zab cde fg
hi jklmno pqrs tu
vwxyz abc de
fgh ijkl mnop qr
stuv wxy zab
cde fg hi jklmno
pqrs tu vwxyz
abc defgh ijkl
mnop qr stuv
wxy zab cde fg
hi jklmno pqrs tu
vwxyz abc def
gh ijkl mnop qr
stuv wxy zab
cde fg hi jklmno
pqrs tu vwxyz

NEWSLETTER II

workflow

search and track

routing

data merge

communications

circle
TECHNOLOGIES

LAYOUT INDEX.206

OVERVIEW

CLIENT
Circle Technologies, a high-tech firm that creates custom software for businesses.

OBJECTIVE
Design a quarterly newsletter that provides current and prospective clients with up-to-date information about the five technical areas that this corporation specializes in.

CONTENT
Mostly text. The product logos are the only available art; they should be used to create visual interest.

AUDIENCE
Wide: from secretarial staff to software engineers and decision makers.

PRODUCTION PARAMETERS
Moderate budget. An effort should be made to find ways to save money.

Newsletter II

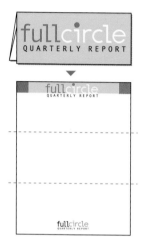

As with the brochure samples featured on pages 42–43, the designs shown here demonstrate how preprinted "masters" (sheets printed in quantity ahead of time) can be "imprinted" on an as-needed basis either by offset press, laser printer or copy machine.

The interior pages featured here are shown with and without a black imprint.

The design formats range from a simple single-column "letter" (left), to more complicated column constructions (right).

Preprinted masters and imprints

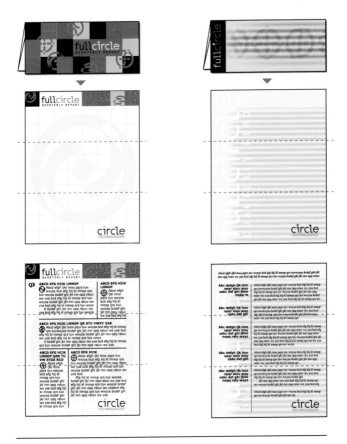

Newsletter II

Limited to two colors? Never underestimate the impact that can be achieved when the right colors are applied to a powerful design. Sometimes limitation is a designer's ally.

EXPLORE: HEAVY INK COVERAGE, BASIC COLORS, BIG IMAGES, BLANK SPACE

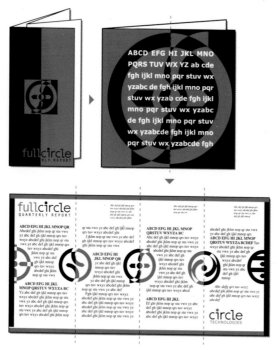

Two-color design

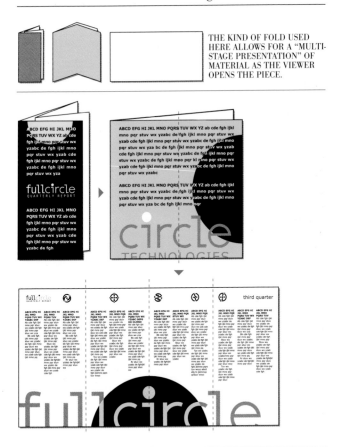

THE KIND OF FOLD USED HERE ALLOWS FOR A "MULTI-STAGE PRESENTATION" OF MATERIAL AS THE VIEWER OPENS THE PIECE.

Newsletter II

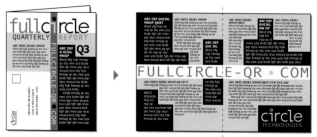

Above: investigate reversed text; consider ignoring the conventional wisdom that advises against it.

EXPLORE: WHITE OR COLORED TYPE, VARIED FONT COLORS AND SIZES, UNUSUAL COLUMN DIMENSIONS AND ARRANGEMENTS.

Above: explore options that defy rules regarding "normal" column shapes, sizes and arrangements.

EXPLORE COLUMNS THAT:
FIT WITHIN SHAPES, CURVE, FOLLOW IRREGULAR LINES
PUSH THE LIMITS OF LEGIBILITY (IF THE PROJECT ALLOWS)

Reversed text, unusual columns, alternatives to paper

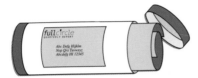

Are there other ways of delivering your message? Investigate different printing formats and methods of packaging and distributing.

If circulation is minimal and/or a budget is large, perhaps you can forget paper entirely and provide clients with a CD that contains interactive media.

When circulation is extremely large, or when the base of recipients is ever-changing, a Web-posted newsletter might be a good option.

FOCUS ON

Grid

A grid is the underlying framework on which some layouts are built. A grid usually defines the number and placement of columns on a page. Text, images and graphics are placed along and within these guidelines.

Designing a specific grid (or set of grids) for use within a multipage piece is a means of promoting a look of continuity from one page to another.

Sometimes grids are followed closely. At other times they are "interrupted" by visual elements. Some layouts do not use grids at all (see pages 218–219).

BELOW: A PAGE-LAYOUT THAT USES A THREE-COLUMN GRID THAT IS INTERRUPTED BY A ONE-COLUMN SECTION IN THE CENTER.

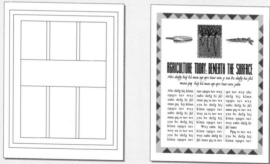

TOP: A GRID DESIGNED FOR A NEWSLETTER THAT INCORPORATES
FOUR DIFFERENT COLUMN ARRANGEMENTS.
BOTTOM: THE GRID IS FILLED—SOMEWHAT LOOSELY— WITH TEXT,
IMAGES AND GRAPHIC ELEMENTS.

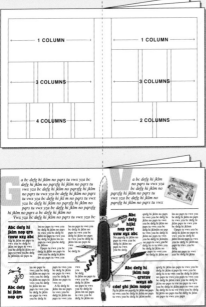

More grid examples are featured on the following page.

FOCUS ON Grid (continued)

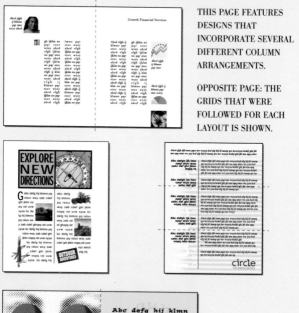

THIS PAGE FEATURES DESIGNS THAT INCORPORATE SEVERAL DIFFERENT COLUMN ARRANGEMENTS.

OPPOSITE PAGE: THE GRIDS THAT WERE FOLLOWED FOR EACH LAYOUT IS SHOWN.

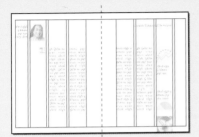

FOCUS ON

Layout Without Grid

Layouts need not be composed according to a grid. Some layouts simply rely on a designer's instinct for their construction.

It is impossible to say how this instinct is developed from one designer to the next, but it could be argued that in most cases, design instinct arises through a combination of seeing, thinking and doing.

So: See; think; do; design.

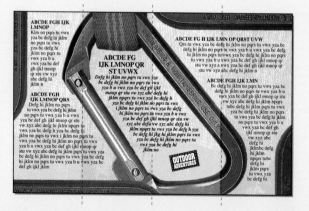

URBAN**DESIGN**INSTITUTE

NEWSLETTER III

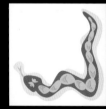

North Park Zoo

OVERVIEW

CLIENT
North Park Zoo.

OBJECTIVE
Produce a colorful, exciting piece that a pre-teen audience will want to read and possibly use as posted art.

CONTENT
This month's newsletter features illustrations centered around a "Summer Safari" theme. Text should be informative and brief. Piece could contain interactive elements such as word games, puzzles or cut-outs.

AUDIENCE
The "Zoo Review," is aimed toward a pre-teen audience.

PRODUCTION PARAMETERS
Fairly large budget. A full-color poster.

Newsletter III

Newsletter as poster

Three designs that are produced as large-format posters. For mailing, these designs could contain printed postal information on the back cover or could be sent in an envelope.

EXPLORE AND CONSIDER:
BIG TEXT
BIG IMAGES
BACKGROUND COLORS
BACKGROUND IMAGES OR PATTERNS
CONTEMPORARY FONTS
COLORFUL TEXT
TEXT BASELINES THAT CURVE
TILTED TEXT
FONTS THAT VARY PER HEADLINE
FONTS THAT VARY PER ARTICLE
TEXT THAT WRAPS AROUND IMAGES
TEXT THAT OVERPRINTS IMAGES
IMAGES THAT RELATE TO ARTICLES
IMAGES THAT FLOAT LOOSELY
ACTIVE BORDERS
BORDERS OF TEXT
COLORFUL BORDERS
LINEWORK, SIMPLE OR ACTIVE

Newsletter III

Give the newsletter's recipient a reason to keep the piece after reading it: provide them with an interesting reverse-side image that might be used as wall art or a book cover.

Consider offering a different image with each issue.

Reverse-side impact

Below and below right: how about a design that offers several pieces of potential keepsake art?

Below left: investigate ways of presenting articles in small, "easy-to-digest" blocks of information.

Newsletter III

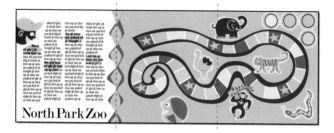

Above and below: interiors for the cover at left.

Games or other interactive goodies might be effective when targeting a young audience.

Youthful readers are usually open to "alternative" typographic solutions.

Interactive features for kids

INTERACTIVE PAGES, CONSIDER:
BOARD GAMES
MASKS
CUT-OUT EYEWEAR
CUT-OUT IMAGES
PUZZLES
COLORING BOOK IMAGES
MAZES
CONNECT-THE-DOTS PICTURES
WORD SEARCH PUZZLES
CROSSWORD PUZZLES
WORD SCRAMBLES
PAPER FIGURINES WITH ACCESSORIES
INSTRUCTIONS FOR ART PROJECTS
SCIENCE EXPERIMENTS
LISTS OF INDOOR AND OUTDOOR ACTIVITIES
LISTS OF INTERESTING FACTS

LOOK THROUGH CHILDREN'S BOOKS AND
MAGAZINES FOR IDEAS.

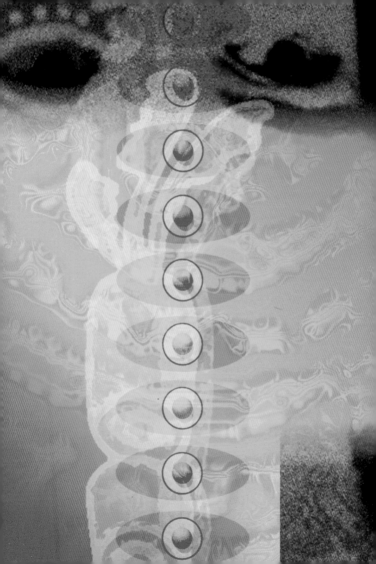

chapter 7

PAGE LAYOUT

Designing a page or page spread(s), whether for a single article or the span of an entire publication, usually involves taking certain production parameters into consideration from the start. The number of inks available, the stock being printed on and the quality of the printing process being used are most often factors determined by a budget that is beyond the designer's control.

Sometimes there are also certain graphic guidelines regarding formats that need to be adhered to. It's a good idea to make sure that you are aware of any restrictions that need to be followed before beginning work on a page layout for a publication or booklet.

Restrictions aside, however, there is

always room for creativity when it comes to page layout. In fact, few forms of media are nearer the cutting edge of design fashion than the pages laid out for progressive magazines, whether they are high gloss, full-color publications or black-and-white newsprint weeklies. Look through publications whose content relates to the subject matter you are working with—especially if you are not completely familiar with the topic so that you can gain a better understanding of the audience's tastes and expectations.

Any of the chapters of this book offer ideas that could be applied to page layout. Check out the *Focus on Grids*, pages 214-215—these concepts apply directly to most page design projects.

PAGE LAYOUT I

star gumball company

OVERVIEW

CLIENT
Star Gumball Company.

OBJECTIVE
Present layout ideas for the nonfinancial section of the company's annual report. The design should enforce Star Gumball's progressive image.

CONTENT
Colorful three-dimensional images of gumballs should be used to complement the text. The design needs to convey the company's upbeat marketing approach, yet be restrained enough to present Star Gumball as a viable financial investment.

AUDIENCE
Adults interested in the company's marketing and financial performance.

PRODUCTION PARAMETERS
Full color, 9" x 12" (22.9cm x 30.5cm) folded.

Page Layout I

A trio of image-heavy designs with unconventional text layouts.

EXPLORE AND CONSIDER:
COLOR!
CONTRASTING SIZES
CONTRASTING STYLES
FULL BLEEDS
BLANK SPACE
TEXT OVER IMAGES
WRAPPED TEXT
TEXT/IMAGE ECHOES

Double page spreads, image heavy, text heavy

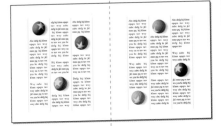

Three text-heavy layouts.

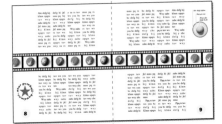

EXPLORE AND CONSIDER:

COLUMNS

TYPESIZE

TYPE WEIGHT

TYPE LEADING

TYPE COLOR

MIXED FONTS

SERIF

SANS SERIF

ITALIC

SCRIPT

NOVELTY

HANDWRITTEN

"EMPTY" COLUMNS

IMAGE-ONLY COLUMNS

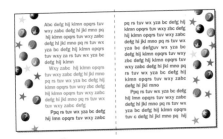

Page Layout I

Take advantage of occasions when there are little or no restrictions on space: consider allowing large images to dominate a page.

Large image, layered image

Search for ways of altering existing images or combining them with other pieces of art to create intriguing visuals.

Explore both electronic and "traditional" methods of altering images.

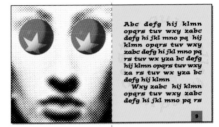

Page Layout I

The two sets of layouts featured on this spread provide examples of how visual themes can be used to establish continuity between spreads.

The spreads on this page rely on a circular element within the text area and large illustrations to define a theme.

The text-heavy layouts on the opposite page are visually connected through a common border treatment, large initial caps, rectangular text "pull-outs" and free-floating gumballs throughout the text area.

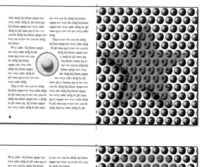

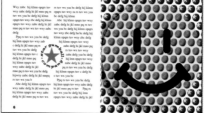

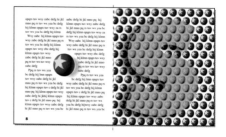

Following theme, sequential pages

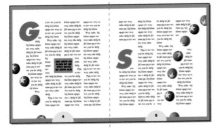

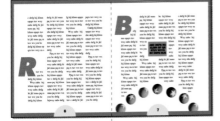

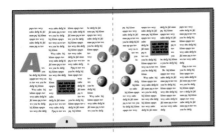

FOCUS ON

Alignment

One way of adding structure to a page is by incorporating subtle and not-so-subtle alignments between elements.

THIS FLOATING BLOCK OF TEXT FEELS ANCHORED BECAUSE OF ITS RELATIONSHIP WITH THE IMAGE ON THE OPPOSITE PAGE.

The examples shown on these pages demonstrate how certain alignments between images, text and graphic elements help give a page a degree of order, even when a page is full of diverse visual material.

Conversely, purposely avoiding alignments between elements, or selectively choosing *which* elements to align, is a way of creating visual tension: an appropriate solution for some projects.

THE "GROUND-LINE" PROVIDES A GOOD CUE FOR THE HEADLINE'S PLACEMENT, BOTH VISUALLY AND CONCEPTUALLY.

THE LETTERHEAD/FLYER SHOWN BELOW (FROM THE FLYER CHAPTER, PAGES 154–155) PROVIDES A MORE COMPLEX EXAMPLE. NOTE HOW THE IMPRINTED ELEMENTS ON THE FLYER AT RIGHT ALIGN SELECTIVELY WITH THE PREPRINTED ELEMENTS ON THE ORIGINAL LETTERHEAD (LEFT).

PAGE LAYOUT II

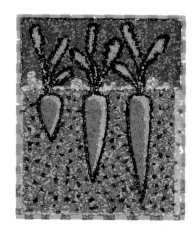

OVERVIEW

CLIENT
Progressive magazine featuring an article on the agriculture industry.

OBJECTIVE
Create a page layout for an article that highlights issues facing the agriculture industry.

CONTENT
Three illustrations that relate to the text have been created for this article. All or some of the images may be used. The opening spread could feature large or small amounts of text since the article will be allowed to flow to other pages.

AUDIENCE
Educated, reasonably progressive readers.

PRODUCTION PARAMETERS
Full color, full page or double page.

Page Layout II

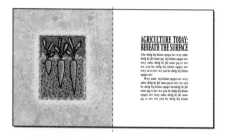

Text and image relationships, spanning pages

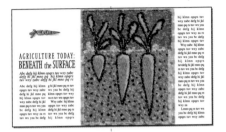

EXPLORE AND CONSIDER:

COLUMNS AND COLUMN ARRANGEMENTS

IMAGE AND TEXT ON OPPOSING PAGES

IMAGES THAT SPAN PAGES

IMAGES THAT INTERRUPT TEXT

IMAGES THAT SEPARATE HEADLINES FROM TEXT

TEXT BLOCKS THAT ECHO AN IMAGE'S SHAPE OR CONTENT

TEXT THAT REVERSES FROM AN IMAGE

FONTS THAT ECHO OR CONTRAST WITH AN IMAGE'S STYLE

Page Layout II

Extremely horizontal illustrations need not be difficult to work with. These five layouts take advantage of the unusual proportions of the featured illustration.

EXPLORE AND CONSIDER:

IMAGES AND/OR HEADLINES THAT SPAN PAGES

IMAGES AND/OR HEADLINES THAT FILL AN ENTIRE PAGE

IMAGES THAT PROVIDE A "BRIDGE" BETWEEN ELEMENTS ON OPPOSITE PAGES

BORDER TREATMENTS THAT HELP HOLD A PAGE SPREAD TOGETHER

Be aware of the potential pitfalls of "jumping gutters" (spanning opposite pages with an image or text): alignment between pages is difficult and elements tend to get "swallowed" in the gap.

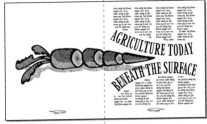

AGRICULTURE TODAY: BENEATH THE SURFACE

ABCD EFG HIJK LM NO PQ RST UV WXY ZABC defg hi jkl mno pq hij klmn opqrs tuv wxy zabc defg hi jkl mno pq rs tuv wx yza bc defg hij klmn opqrs tuv

Wxy zabc hij klmn opqrs tuv wxy zabc defg hi jkl mno pq rs tuv wx yza bc defg hij klmn opqrs tuv wx defg hij klmn opqrs tuv wxy zabc

bc defg hij klmn opqrs tuv wxy zabc defg hi jkl mno pq rs tuv wx yza bc defg hij klmn opqrs tuv wx

Wxy zabc hij klmn opqrs tuv wxy zabc defg hi jkl mno pq rs tuv wx yza bc defg hij klmn opqrs tuv wx defg hij klmn opqrs tuv wxy zabc defg hi jkl mno pq rs tuv wx yza bc defg hij klmn opqrs tuv wx

AGRICULTURE TODAY: BENEATH THE SURFACE

G be defg hij klmn opqrs tuv wxy zabc defg hi jkl mno pq rs tuv wx yza bc defg hij klmn opqrs tuv

Wxy zabc hij klmn opqrs tuv wxy zabc defg hi jkl mno pq rs tuv wx yza bc defg hij klmn opqrs tuv

Ppq rs tuv wx yza bc defg hij klmn opqrs tuv wxy zabc defg hij klmn opqrs tuv wxy zabc

be defg hij klmn opqrs tuv wxy zabc defg hi jkl klmn opqrs tuv wxy zabc defg hi jkl mno pq rs tuv wx

Wya be defg hij klmn opqrs tuv wxy zabc defg hi jkl mno pq rs tuvwdefg hij klmn opqrs tuv wx yza bc defg hij klmn opqrs tuv wxy zabc defg hi jkl mno pq rs tuv wx yza bc defghijk lmno pqrs Lmno pq rs tuv wx yza bc defg hij klmn opqrs tuv wxy zabc defg hi jkl mno pq rs tuv wx yza bc defg hij klmn opqrs tuv wxy zabc defg hij klmn opqrs tuv wxy zabc defg

AGRICULTURE TODAY: BENEATH THE SURFACE

Abc defg hij kl mn op qrs tuv wx y za bc defg hi jkl mno pq hij kl mn op qrs tuv wx yde

Abc defg hi jkl mno pq klmn opqrs tuv wx yza bc defg hij klmn opqrs tuv wxy za rs tuv wx yza bc defg hij klmn opqrs tuv

Wxy zabc hij klmn opqrs tuv wxy zabc defg hi jkl mno pq rs tuv wx yza bc defg hij klmn opqrs tuvwdefg hi jkl mno pq rs tuv wx yza bc defg hij klmn opqrs tuv wxy zabc defg hi jkl mno pq rs tuv wx yza bc defg hij klmn opqrs tuv wxy

Lmno pq rs tuv wx yza bc defg hij klmn opqrs tuv wxy zabc defg hij klmn opqrs tuv wxy zabc defg hi jkl mno pq rs tuv wx yza bc defg hij klmn opqrs tuv wxy zabc defg hij klmn opqrs tuv wxy zabc defg hij klmn opqrs tuv wxy zabc defg hij klmn opqrs tuv wxy zabc defg hij klmn opqrs tuv wxy zabc defg hij klmn opqrs tuv wxy zabc defg hi mno pq rs tuv wx yza bc

AGRICULTURE TODAY: BENEATH THE SURFACE

G abc defg hij jkl mno pq hij klmn opqrs tuv wxy zabc defg hi jkl mno pq rs tuv wx yza bc defg hij klmn opqrs tuv wxy za rs tuv wx yza bc defg hij klmn opqrs tuv

Wxy zabc hij klmn opqrs tuv wxy zabc defg hi jkl mno pq rs tuv wx yza bc defg hij klmn opqrs tuv

defg hij jkl mno pq rs tuv wx yza bc defg hij klmn opqrs tuv wx yza bc defg hij klmn opqrs tuv

Wxy zabc hij klmn opqrs tuv wxy zabc defg hi jkl mno pq rs tuv wx yza bc defg hij klmn opqrs tuv klmn opqrs tuv wxy zabc defg hi jkl mno pq rs tuv wx yza bc defg hij klmn opqrs tuv

Satuv wx yza bc defg hij klmn opqrs tuv wxy zabc defg hi jkl mno pq rs tuv wx yza bc defg hij klmn opqrs tuv

klmn opqrs tuv wxy za rs tuv wx yza bc defg hij klmn opqrs tuv wxy zabc defg hij klmn opqrs tuv wxy zabc defg hi jkl mno pq rs tuv wx yza bc defg hij klmn opqrs tuv wxy za

jkl mno pq rs tuv wx yza bc defg hij klmn opqrs tuv wxy zabc defg hij klmn opqrs tuv wxy zabc defg hi jkl mno pq rs tuv wx yza bc defg hij klmn opqrs tuv

Lmno pq rs tuv wx yza bc defg hij klmn opqrs tuv wxy zabc defg hij klmn opqrs tuv wxy zabc defg hi jkl mno pq rs tuv

Abc defg hij kl mn op tuv wx y za bc defg hijkl mno pq hij kl mn op

Text and image relationships, single page

Single-page layouts:

EXPLORE AND CONSIDER:
ACTIVE BORDER TREATMENTS
COLORFUL HEADS OR FEATURED TEXT
CONTRASTING FONTS
CONDENSED HEADLINE FONT
EXPANDED HEADLINE FONT
TEXT-HEAVY LAYOUT
IMAGE-HEAVY LAYOUT

*Experiment by giving visual
emphasis to different elements.*

Typographic layouts

Type-only layouts:

Opposite page: double-page layouts that use visual effects, color and layers to conceptually tie in with the story's topic. Use of color, shading and/or well considered typography can compensate for a lack of photos or illustrations.

This page: single-page layouts that also utilizes a visual tie in. While this article seems to call for such a connection, others may not.

How far can legibility be pushed with the audience you are designing for?

Are visual/conceptual tie-ins called for?

Not a Photographer?
Not a Problem.

Featured on this spread are two alternatives to using a camera to capture photos for use as illustration material.

Left: an image downloaded from a stock photo source. Below: the same photo following treatment in Adobe Photoshop, with a final result far removed from the original image.

Another method of image capture/alteration is shown on the opposite page.

The image above was created by scanning four rose stems using a desktop scanner.

The image was then adjusted (right, top to bottom): colorized, treated and combined with an image of a pile of nails (also "photographed" using a desktop scanner).

PAGE LAYOUT III

OVERVIEW

CLIENT
Progressive magazine featuring an article on body art.

OBJECTIVE
Produce a visually intriguing layout that focuses on the cultural and personal factors surrounding the decision to permanently decorate the body.

CONTENT
A single piece of art has been created for this piece. Typography should echo the illustration's contemporary feel.

AUDIENCE
Late teens through early 30s. Progressive.

PRODUCTION PARAMETERS
Full color. Explore layout ideas that are both image heavy and text heavy for the opening spread.

Page Layout III

Conventional "rules" of layout
and legibility can be stretched
when addressing an audience
with a progressive mindset. It may
be permissible to offer a message
that is challenging to uncover,
along with text that is somewhat
difficult to read.

The task facing designers here lies
in finding just the right balance
between anarchy and order.

EXPLORE AND CONSIDER:
REVERSED TEXT
CONTEMPORARY FONTS
TEXT FILLED WITH IMAGES OR PATTERNS
LAYERS OF TEXT AND IMAGES
CONTEMPORARY ILLUSTRATION STYLES
CONTEMPORARY COLOR SCHEMES
UNUSUAL COLUMN ARRANGEMENTS

Stretching convention, reversed text

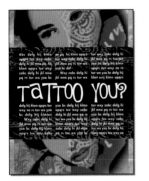

Above and below: layouts might appeal to certain viewers through the use of unusual croppings, image treatments, headline treatments, column arrangements and white space.

Right: designs that feature a background pattern/image that was created from a portion of the featured photo. A background can visually connect stylistically different elements or elements that are on opposing pages. Backgrounds can also soften the contrast between images, text and the paper they are printed on.

Image alteration, background treatment

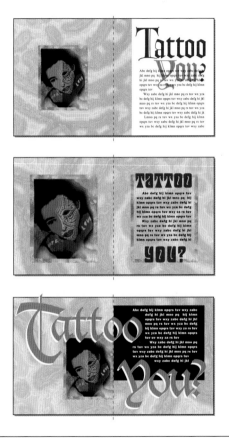

Page Layout III

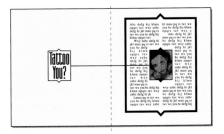

Above and below: designs that make use of empty space to draw attention to the featured text and image.

Left: layouts that "bombard" the viewer with visuals. Layers of text, images and color can be used to create a collage of relevant material. Consider exploring these ideas with image-altering software or through traditional "hands-on" techniques and media.

FOCUS ON

The Golden Mean

The Golden Mean is relationship between sizes that is pleasing to the human eye. Why? Who knows. Perhaps it's because proportions that follow the Golden Mean exist everywhere in nature, and have been used by artists both instinctively and by plan for centuries.

Many designers intentionally use these proportions when designing a page. Below is an example of such a design—the measurements

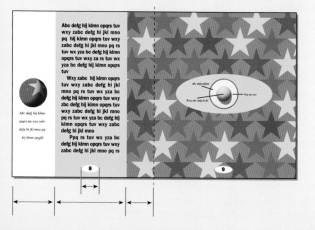

noted below the layout follow the proportions of the Golden Mean.

What are these proportions and how are they derived? Basically, the Golden Mean is a set of numbers (also known as the Fibonacci series):

2, 3, 5, 8, 13, 21, 34, 55, 89, 144, 233...

To understand this sequence, simply note that each number is the sum of the two that come before it.

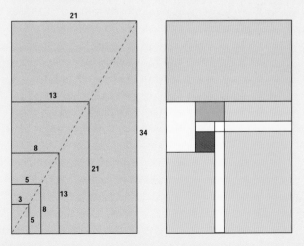

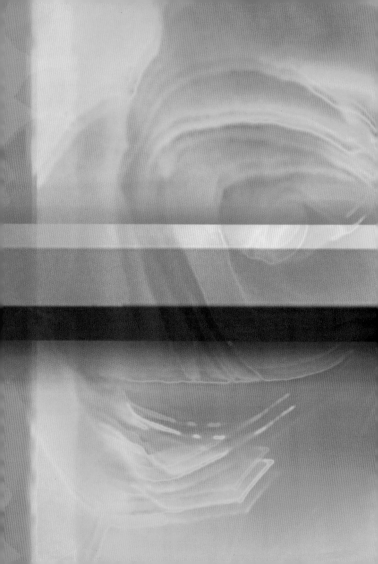

STATIONERY

chapter 8

STATIONERY

In Western society, our clothing, hairstyle, home and automobile are among the items that tell others who we (supposedly) are. And while some people are able to live without being influenced by the opinions of others, most of us tend to make choices (clothing, hair, etc.) that underscore the fact that we, to some degree or another, are aware of the tendency of people to judge one another based on outward appearance.

What has this got to with stationery? Quite a bit. Stationery is a company's way of telling others who they are. Often, designers and clients underestimate the power they have over the perception of others when they create an organization's stationery. Try this: rather than thinking in terms of producing stationery that reflects the way a company sees itself, think along the lines of "How do they want others to see them?"

Also, it's worth noting here that it's considerably easier to push the associations between perception and reality with stationery than it is in real life. An overweight man might be dubiously judged if seen wearing a bikini at the beach, but a well-designed business card for a two-person company operating from an unfinished basement can leave its recipient with the same (or better) impression than a card from multimillion-dollar corporation.

Search for the best possible visual and tactile vocabulary of color, layout, typography and paper to tell the world who the client is.

STATIONERY

BODY LOTION

OVERVIEW

CLIENT
This section features stationery packages for several of the clients featured elsewhere in this book.

OBJECTIVE
Design a letterhead, business card and envelope for each client. In each case, the three pieces should relate visually to each other. Throughout this section, a wide range of style and budget considerations are presented.

CONTENT
In each case, the client's logo should be featured. Additional elements that support the company's image may be featured as well.

PRODUCTION PARAMETERS
In most cases, standard measurements are followed: letterheads are 8.5" x 11" (21.6cm x 27.9cm); business cards measure 3.5" x 2" (8.9cm x 5.1cm); and envelopes are 9.5" x 4.125" (24.1cm x 10.5cm).

Stationery

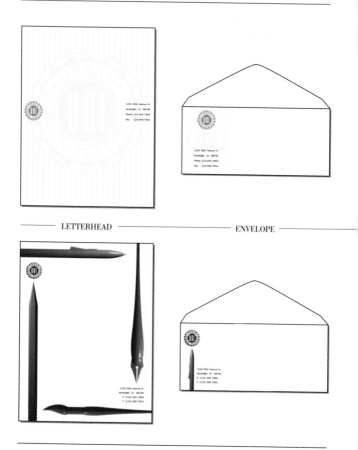

LETTERHEAD ——————————— ENVELOPE ——————————

Backgrounds, images

A three-color design that makes use of a background treatment to visually tie the separate pieces together. If budget restrictions do not allow for more than one or two ink colors, consider using screen tints in the background image.

EXPLORE AND CONSIDER:
EMBLEM, SEAL
BACKGROUND PATTERN
BACKGROUND IMAGE
BACKGROUND COLOR, SOLID OR SCREENED
GRADUATED TINTS

Consider using images as part of a design.

The images shown with these layouts are duotones (black plus one other ink color).

EXPLORE AND CONSIDER:
IMAGES THAT BLEED
IMAGES THAT DO NOT BLEED
MULTIPLE IMAGES
FULL COLOR, DUOTONE
BLACK AND WHITE

Stationery

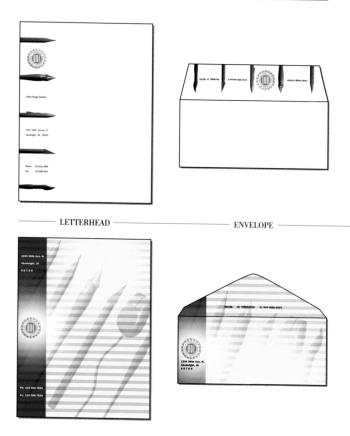

LETTERHEAD ——— ENVELOPE

Consider using images or graphic elements as dividers between text elements.

Also think about restricting the use of color to all or part of a single element.

Jane A. Smith
Executive Director

Urban Design Institute

1234 56th Avenue N.
Abcdefghi, JK 98765
Phone: 123.456.7890
Fax: 123.098.7654

BUSINESS CARD

A more expensive package: full color and full bleed on all items. Two concerns to be aware of when printing background images on a letterhead: the image needs to be light enough to allow the overprinting letter to be easily read, and a background image can sometimes interfere with the legibility of faxed documents.

Stationery

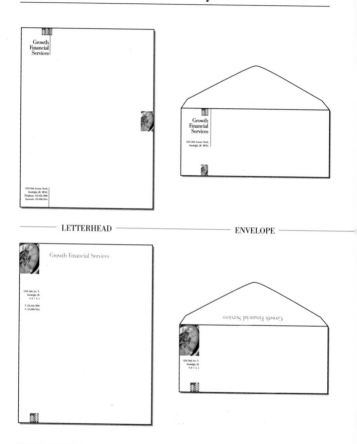

LETTERHEAD

ENVELOPE

Unconventional placement and proportion

Explore "unconventional" placements and sizes for graphic elements.

EXPLORE AND CONSIDER:
IMAGES THAT ECHO LOGO
IMAGES THAT BLEED
HORIZONTAL/VERTICAL IMAGES
CARD: HORIZONTAL? VERTICAL?
COLOR/B&W/DUOTONE IMAGES
PAPER OPTIONS

Growth
Financial
Services

Jane A. Smith
Executive Director
1234 56th Avenue North
Abcdefghi, JK 98765
Telephone: 123.456.7890
Facsimile: 123.098.7654

BUSINESS CARD

Think about using an image as the dominant element in a design. Investigate different placement options for each element.

Jane A. Smith
Executive Director
1234 56th Avenue North
Abcdefghi, JK 98765
Telephone: 123.456.7890
Facsimile: 123.098.7654

Growth Financial Services

Stationery

BACK ▶

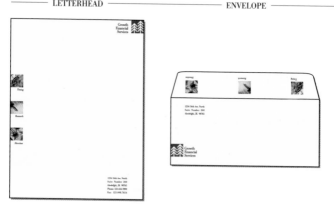

LETTERHEAD

ENVELOPE

When a budget permits, consider more elaborate presentations.

◀ BACK

Growth Financial Services

JANE A. SMITH, EXECUTIVE DIRECTOR

1234 56TH AVE. N., NUMBER 260, ABCDEFGHI, JK 98765

PHONE: 123.456.7890, FAX: 123.098.7654

BUSINESS CARD

"Visual rhythm" is the theme here: the proportions of the company's icon is echoed throughout the designs.

Consider using white, off-white, ivory and gray papers for corporate clients.

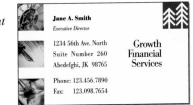

Jane A. Smith
Executive Director

1234 56th Ave. North
Suite Number 260
Abcdefghi, JK 98765

Phone: 123.456.7890
Fax: 123.098.7654

Growth
Financial
Services

Stationery

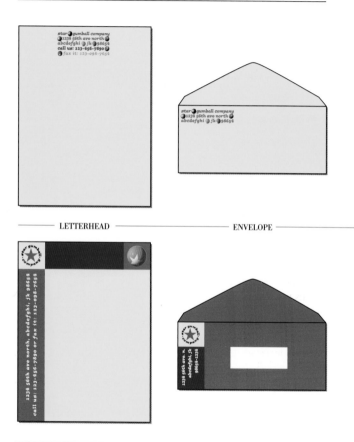

LETTERHEAD ——————————— ENVELOPE

Why be normal? Non-conventional clients call for nonconventional solutions. The following stationery sets explore a few of the countless ways that convention can be stretched and ignored.

BUSINESS CARD

EXPLORE AND CONSIDER:
COLOR!
SOLID OR TINTED COLOR
SCREEN BUILDS
UNUSUAL IMAGES
INTERESTING IMAGE CROPPING
REPETITIVE IMAGES
UNEXPECTED PLACEMENT
TYPOGRAPHIC OPTIONS
ONE FONT OR SEVERAL
REVERSE TYPE
COLOR TYPE
MULTICOLOR TYPE

Stationery

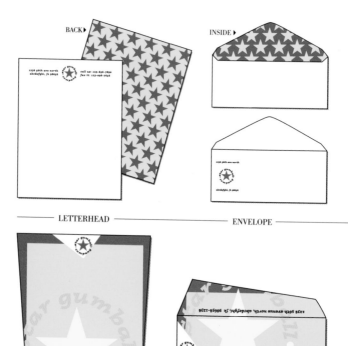

BACK ▶

INSIDE ▶

1238 56th ave north
abcdefghi, jk 98658

call us: 123-456-7890
fax is: 123-456-7896

1238 56th ave north

abcdefghi, jk 98658

——— LETTERHEAD ———

——— ENVELOPE ———

1238 56th avenue north, abcdefghi, jk 98658-1238

1238 56th avenue north, abcdefghi, jk 98658-1238

Folding card, nonsquare trimming

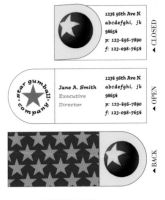

An unusual die cut and fold can result in a hard-to-ignore business card.

Note that the back side pattern on each of these items is "the-same-but-different": the pattern stays the same, while the colors change for each item.

◀ CLOSED

◀ OPEN

◀ BACK

Jane A. Smith
Executive
Director

1234 56th Ave N.
abcdefghi, jk
98654
p: 123-456-7890
f: 123-098-7654

star gumball company

BUSINESS CARD

Don't be square: unusual dimensions are a good way to break away from the crowd.

Layering elements is a way of achieving a rich visual presentation.

Jane A. Smith
Executive Director

1234 56th avenue north
abcdefghi, jk 98654
call us: 123-456-7890
fax it: 123-098-7654

star gumball company

Stationery

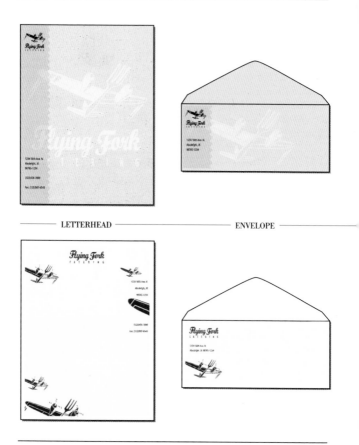

LETTERHEAD ———————— ENVELOPE

Opaque ink, background screen

A three-color design that includes an opaque white ink. A subtle variation between the pieces is achieved by using slightly different shades of the same stock.

EXPLORE AND CONSIDER:
PAPER OPTIONS
OPAQUE INKS
LAYERS OF IMAGES AND TEXT

BUSINESS CARD

A black-plus-one-color design that mimics the effect of the opaque white used in the samples above (the white in these designs is achieved by reversing from the background screen). Note that none of these designs bleed—a cost-saving measure.

EXPLORE AND CONSIDER:
BACKGROUND COLORS OR TINTS
REPETITIVE ELEMENTS
ELEMENTS THAT BLEED
UNUSUAL TYPE PLACEMENT

Stationery

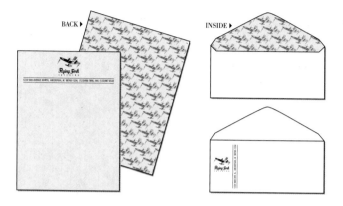

BACK ▶

INSIDE ▶

PRESS SHEET: DOUBLE-SIDED LETTERHEAD.

BOTH THE FRONT AND BACK OF A TWO-SIDED LETTERHEAD CAN BE PRINTED IN A SINGLE PRESS RUN IF THE SHEET IS TURNED OVER AND RUN THROUGH FOR A SECOND PASS. THE SHEET WOULD BE TRIMMED AFTERWARDS.

If corporate standards allow, a repetitive pattern created from a company's logo can provide an interesting background. See below for ideas on using press sheets efficiently for these effects.

BACK ◄

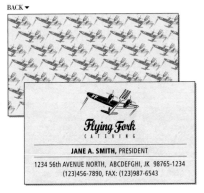

PRESS SHEET: DOUBLE-SIDED BUSINESS CARD.

AS WITH THE LETTER-HEAD'S PRESS SHEET (OPPOSITE PAGE), THE PRESS SHEET IS RUN THROUGH THE PRESS ONCE, TURNED OVER, AND RUN AGAIN. THE FINAL PIECES ARE THEN CUT FROM THE SHEET.

FOCUS ON

Listening to the Client

Note that the title of this Focus is not *"Hearing* the Client." Hearing is what your ears and mind do as they process the voices and sounds made by a crowd of people at a gallery while the rest of the mind focuses on the painting in front of you. *Listening* is the intentional act of trying to understand what a particular person is saying and what their words mean.

A fine distinction, but important when you consider how easy it is to merely hear a client's words during a meeting as opposed to listening for the significance of those words.

Additionally, even if you are very clear on what a client has said during a conversation, it is critical to be sure that you understand the true meaning of the words they use to define their expectations. An example: a client tells you, "I want my stationery to look modern."

Modern? What do they mean? The word

modern might carry a very different meaning to a designer who is immersed daily in the ever-changing fashions of the profession than it does to a client whose expertise may lie elsewhere.

To avoid wasted time and the risk of presenting the client with misdirected layouts, you need to make an assessment of what words and concepts like this mean to them—*ask for their definitions*. It might also be useful to look at printed pieces or the Web for examples of work that they like, as well for examples of design they don't care for. Look around their office: what kind of art have they posted? How *modern* are their surroundings? How *modern* are the clothes and jewelry they are wearing? Any clues there? Listen, then, with all of your senses—give your creative instincts and your logical mind plenty of fuel to work with as you begin a new project.

Stationery

LETTERHEAD — ENVELOPE

Consider using a stock that comes with an uneven "deckled" edge.

Featured image, fold-over card

If the budget allows, and an interesting image is available, consider using an image on stationery.

Explore interesting ways of combining image and text.

A fold-over business card with an intentionally vague cover.

Stationery

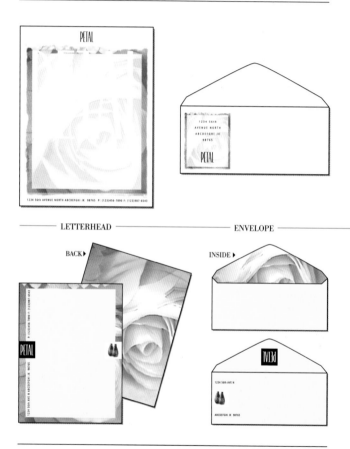

LETTERHEAD — ENVELOPE

BACK ▶

INSIDE ▶

Consider applying a consistent border treatment within each piece as a way of establishing theme.

EXPLORE AND CONSIDER:
BORDERS THAT BLEED, BORDERS THAT DO NOT
JAGGED OR BLURRED EDGES ON A BORDER
IMAGES OR PATTERNS WITHIN BORDERS
ORNATE BORDERS
LINEWORK THAT IS USED AS A BORDER
SUBTLE BORDERS, BOLD BORDERS
BORDERS MADE OF WORDS
BORDERS MADE OF REPETITIVE IMAGES

BUSINESS CARD

Unlike the example above, the border treatment used on the letterhead here is not applied to the other pieces. Rather, the theme is carried by a consistent use of a large image printed on the reverse side of each item.

Stationery

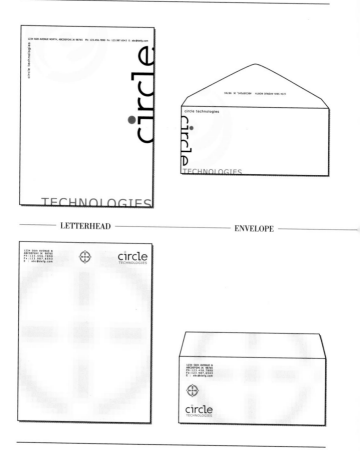

LETTERHEAD ———————— ENVELOPE

No photos or illustrations are used in these layouts—look for interesting ways to effectively use existing icons and typography.

Note that there is no definite "right-side up" on this business card.

BUSINESS CARD

EXPLORE AND CONSIDER:
GHOSTED BACKGROUND IMAGES
BLURRED BACKGROUND IMAGES
REPETITIVE IMAGES
IMAGES OR TYPE THAT BLEED
PATTERNS MADE FROM IMAGES
TYPOGRAPHY THAT IS USED AS A FOCAL POINT
TYPE: LARGE? SMALL? LIGHT? DARK? FONT?
VARIED ORIENTATION OF ELEMENTS
RESTRAINED USE OF ACCENT COLOR
HIGH-IMPACT COLOR COMBINATIONS
VARIOUS PAPER CHOICES
DUPLEX STOCK
FOIL, EMBOSSING, DIE CUT, DRILL, VARNISH

Stationery

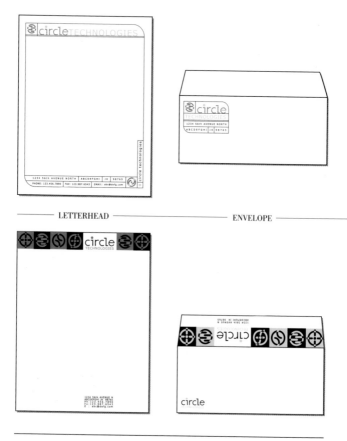

LETTERHEAD

ENVELOPE

Linework—the options are endless and continually subject to changes in fashion.

EXPLORE AND CONSIDER:
ONE WEIGHT OR SEVERAL?
LINE WEIGHT: THICK? THIN?
BLACK LINES? COLORED?
LINES AS A BORDER DEVICE
LINES TO SEPARATE ELEMENTS
STRAIGHT LINES
CURVED LINES
DOTTED/DASHED LINES

circleTECHNOLOGIES

JANE A. SMITH

executive director

1234 56th AVE N	ABCDEFGHI	JK	98765
PHONE : 123.456.7890			
FAX : 123.987.6543			
EMAIL : abc@defg.com			

BUSINESS CARD

JANE A. SMITH
EXECUTIVE DIRECTOR

circle
TECHNOLOGIES

1234 56th AVENUE N
ABCDEFGHI JK 98765
Ph: 123.456.7890
Fx: 123.987.6543
E : abc@defg.com

The use of repetitive symbols establishes a connection between these pieces, even though the symbols are presented differently on each item.

BACK ▶

Stationery

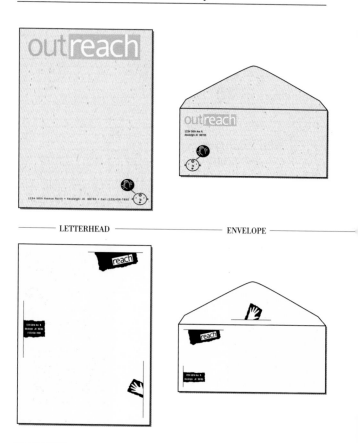

LETTERHEAD   ENVELOPE

Design-on-a-budget: the four sets of layouts shown here are all single color (black), and only the business cards include images that bleed.

A large element (top of letterhead, left) can be softened by printing it in a light screen—a way of achieving impact without overwhelming other elements.

EXPLORE AND CONSIDER:

SINGLE-COLOR PRINTING

BOLD, LARGE IMAGES

SCREEN TINTS

REVERSED TYPE AND/OR IMAGES

CROPPED IMAGES

TILTED OR VERTICAL ELEMENTS

COPY-MACHINE PRINTING

HAND-COLORED ELEMENTS

HAND-DRAWN ELEMENTS

ART THAT IS "RAW, UNREFINED, URBAN"

SIMPLE, CLEAN DESIGN

INTRIGUING PAPER

COLORFUL PAPER

Stationery

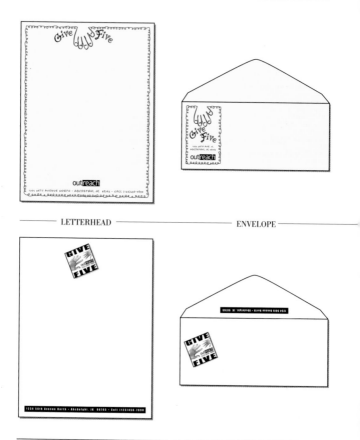

LETTERHEAD

ENVELOPE

Hand crafted, advertising elements

Consider a design that is all or partly hand drawn.

EXPLORE AND CONSIDER:
HAND-DRAWN ART ELEMENTS
HAND-DRAWN BORDERS
VARIOUS STYLES:
    TIGHT? ROUGH? REALISTIC? ABSTRACT?
VARIOUS MEDIA:
    PENCIL, PEN, INK, CHARCOAL, CHALK, PAINT

*What kind of paper would best comple-
ment the style of art you are featuring?*

BUSINESS CARD

*A different approach:
a small-space ad from
page 187 has been used
as the featured element in
this stationery package.*

*Investigate the avail-
ability of ready-to-use
art elements.*

Stationery

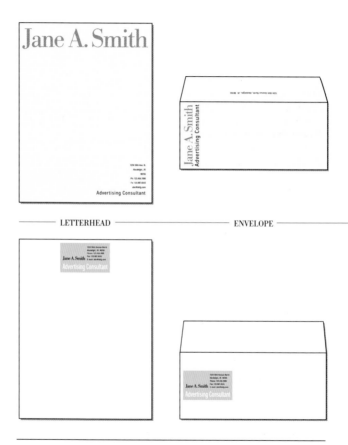

LETTERHEAD

ENVELOPE

*The following designs
(through page 305),
contain mostly
typographic elements.*

*Look for typographic
solutions that complement
the client's "look."*

BUSINESS CARD

*Here, the emphasis has
been placed on the client's
title, rather than their
name (as seen above).
The heavy use of color on
the business card helps
compensate for a lack of
other visual elements.*

*The business card itself is
used as an art element for
the letterhead and
envelope.*

Stationery

BUSINESS CARDS

ROLODEX CARD

This spread features a set of three-color items printed on one card-stock press sheet (shown at left).

Above: consider designing a set of related but different business cards for a client.

POSTCARD (BLANK ON THE REVERSE SIDE)

PRESS SHEET:
THREE-COLOR, ONE-SIDED, CARD STOCK.

FOUR BUSINESS CARDS, A ROLODEX CARD
AND A POSTCARD ARE ALL PRINTED ON A
SINGLE PRESS SHEET.

Stationery

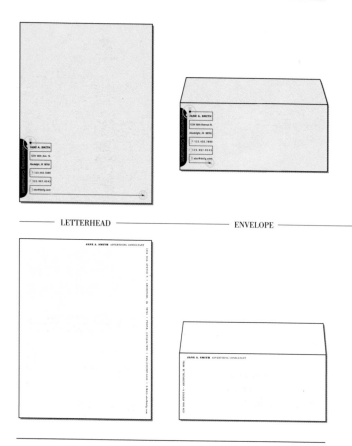

———— LETTERHEAD ———————————————— ENVELOPE ————

Consider complementing a typographic design with simple linework, bars and background elements.

How about a layout that places information around the edges as well as in the center?

Consider printing a very light tint of a color in the background to add tone to a stock.

FOCUS ON

Visual Adhesive

Although the samples shown on this spread are all business cards, the concept presented here can be applied to any form of visual media.

Sometimes "visual adhesive" is called for to hold a design together. Take a look at the business card designs on the facing page. Note how the addition of a light background image or panel helps hold the design together—forming a connection between the scattered elements while adding aesthetic interest at the same time.

Another useful means of bringing elements to order is through the use of linework, as seen with the business card on this page.

Consider using some form of visual adhesive the next time you feel that a layout is lacking interest or not holding itself together.

circleTECHNOLOGIES

JANE A. SMITH

executive director

| 1234 56th AVE N | ABCDEFGHI | JK | 98765 |

PHONE: 123.456.7890

FAX: 123.987.6543

EMAIL: abc@defg.com

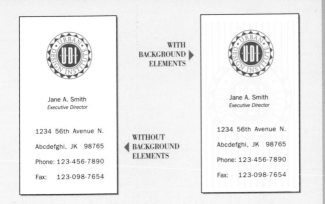

WITH
BACKGROUND
ELEMENTS ▶

◀ WITHOUT
BACKGROUND
ELEMENTS

WITH
BACKGROUND
ELEMENTS ▶

◀ WITHOUT
BACKGROUND
ELEMENTS

Index

*It is my hope that this book will
help designers of all kinds
find ever new ways of adding ink
to paper and pixels to a screen.*

Jim Krause